# Truth and Peace in the Middle East

# Truth and Peace in the Middle East

## A Critical Analysis of the Quaker Report

*by* ARNOLD M. SOLOWAY
*with* EDWIN WEISS *and* GERALD CAPLAN



Published by
FRIENDLY HOUSE PUBLISHERS
NEW YORK
for
THE AMERICAN JEWISH CONGRESS
and
THE ANTI-DEFAMATION LEAGUE OF B'NAI BRITH

SBN 87068-175-3

MANUFACTURED IN THE UNITED STATES OF AMERICA
LIBRARY OF CONGRESS CATALOG CARD NUMBER: 78-172532

## CONTENTS

## ABOUT THE AUTHORS

ARNOLD M. SOLOWAY received his Ph.D. in Economics from Harvard University in 1952. He has taught at Harvard, Boston College and Brown University. In 1965, Dr. Soloway received the Brotherhood Award of the National Conference of Christians and Jews, Northeast Region.

EDWIN WEISS is Professor of Mathematics at Boston University. He has taught at the University of Michigan, Harvard, U.C.L.A., and was a Member of the Institute for Advanced Study, Princeton, New Jersey. Dr. Weiss is a former member of the Executive Committee, American Professors for Peace in the Middle East, Boston Chapter.

GERALD CAPLAN, Senior Psychiatric Consultant for the U.S. Peace Corps, is Professor of Psychiatry at Harvard Medical School. He is also on the Board of Trustees of the Law and Society Association, and Honorary President of the International Association of Child Psychiatry and Allied Professions.

ACKNOWLEDGMENTS

The impetus and encouragement to undertake this critique came from the Special Committee on Israel of the New England Region, American Jewish Congress.

Additional assistance was given by the Jewish Community Council of Metropolitan Boston and the New England Region, Anti-Defamation League of B'nai B'rith.

The development of this critique would not have been possible without an essential memorandum contributed by Professor Ben Halpern, Brandeis University, which provided the basis for most of our comment on the Quaker report's treatment of historical backgrounds.

Valuable and much appreciated editorial and substantive suggestions came from reviews of earlier drafts of the manuscript by Professor John F. Roche, Brandeis University; Joan F. Soloway; Dr. Herbert O. LeVine, Harvard University; Helene M. LeVine; Professor Milton Konvitz, Cornell University; Rabbi Roland B. Gittelsohn; Sumner Z. Kaplan; Richard Cohen, American Jewish Congress; and Stan Wexler, Anti-Defamation League of B'nai B'rith.

Of course, the authors alone are responsible for any deficiencies in the text.

A. M. S.
E. W.
G. C.

## INTRODUCTION

The humanitarian traditions of the Quakers and the deep regard in which they are so widely held by virtue of their long dedication to peace have made many persons understandably reluctant to question the validity and intent of the study prepared for the American and Canadian Friends Service Committees, *Search for Peace in the Middle East* (Fawcett Premier Book). With so many others, we too had assumed that Quakers, especially, would seek to be impartial, fair and objective in their approach to such a complex and controversial subject. But their *Search for Peace in the Middle East* is not such a work. Its authors have, in fact, displayed a blatant bias, repressed facts, distorted history and presented a slanted and one-sided set of conclusions. Their recommendations are, in our view, detrimental to the cause of peace in the Middle East. In this critique we will discuss some of the main arguments of the Quaker report and analyze its conclusions.

We believe, moreover, that the relevance of our critical analysis extends beyond the American Friends Service Committee and the related groups which sponsored the Quaker report. We hope that the facts and analysis which form the substance of our critique may challenge other well-intentioned readers to re-examine the basis of their own assessment of the Middle East crisis.

## CHAPTER I

# IN THE BEGINNING

It was out of their own concern, "and with the urgings of both Jews and Arabs," according to the authors of *Search for Peace in the Middle East,* that a Quaker study group began, in 1968, the exploration of possible approaches to peace in the Middle East. As the back cover reads, ". . . they listened attentively to every point of view and worked carefully through eighteen drafts to arrive at this report. It has been reviewed in detail by many Jews and Arabs . . ." The final paragraph of the preface reads: "We have tried simply to follow the best light we could find toward the most complete truth we could understand."

It would be interesting to know first who were the Jews and the Arabs who urged the Quaker group to undertake this study. But since those parties remain unidentified, we turn instead to some documented observations on how the Quaker group "listened attentively to every point of view," and to the results of the report's review "in detail by many Jews" as the authors followed "the best light . . . toward the most complete truth."

### *The Jerusalem Conference*

Early in 1970, on Quaker initiative, a conference was held between members of the Quaker group, including Landrum R. Bolling, the editor of the report and Paul B. Johnson, Quaker Representative in the Middle East, and several world-renowned legal scholars then resident at the Harry S. Truman Center for the Advancement of Peace, in Jerusalem. The Truman Center group included Professor Julius Stone, University of Sydney (Australia) Faculty of Law; Professor Milton Konvitz, Cornell University School of Law, and Professor Charles Boasson of the Truman Center.

At the time of the conference, the Quakers had already completed their tenth draft. In a detailed critique of that tenth draft, sent to Paul Johnson on February 20, 1970, Professor Stone wrote as follows:

"Dr. Bolling said at our conference on Friday 13th, that he tended to agree with U.S. governmental suggestions that a pro-Arab presentation is required to balance what he claimed was a pro-Israel slant in the mass media.

"How in the light of the above admission as to the background," asked Professor Stone in his critique, "can it be claimed as it is . . . that this Quaker document is making an approach which is 'objective, balanced, candid, realistic?' "

Professor Stone's question was never answered.

Two sentences from the Quaker preface (p. 8) are also worthy of special attention:

"A major obstacle to rational understanding of the Arab-Israeli dilemma is to be found in the polarization of popular attitudes in the West, especially in the United States. This polarization has resulted in frequent distortion of the issues in the press and in other communications media."

These Quaker assertions raise some interesting questions. First, why is "polarization" in the West, "especially in the United States," a greater obstacle to rational understanding than the obviously more extreme polarization in the East, especially in the U.S.S.R.? Second, do the press and other media—which are free in the West—really distort issues to express already polarized popular attitudes? Is it not just possible, in view of the clear record of Arab aggression, intransigent hostility, and refusal to honor commitments, that the Western public has come to sympathize with Israel's struggle for survival? And would it not have been relevant here to discuss the possibly harmful impact on "rational understanding" of the completely government-controlled press and media of the Communist and Arab worlds, where government censors as part of the daily routine distort all sensitive issues to make the flow of public "information" conform with pre-established government positions?

The report's curious comments on the "polarization of popular attitudes" suggests that the Quakers are insinuating the weary and discredited canard that the press and media of the United States are controlled by the Jews and Zionists. The Quakers do charge that Western, and especially American, press and mass media are unduly "pro-Israel." These lines in the report reveal the same basic understanding as that stated by Dr. Landrum Bolling at the Jerusalem conference when he "tended to agree . . . that a pro-Arab slant is required to balance what he claimed was a pro-Israel slant in the mass media."

While further evidence of the Quaker group's pro-Arab slant will be explored later, correspondence between the Quakers and the scholars at the Truman Center following their Jerusalem conference would seem to have some bearing on the basic intent of the Quaker effort. Following are excerpts from a series of letters that bear on the issue of the Quaker group's good faith:

*From letter of March 19, 1970; Professor Stone to Paul B. Johnson:*

"Your letter opens with a statement of thanks 'for the enormous effort in commenting so carefully upon Draft Ten of the Quaker statement on the Middle East.' This naturally led me to expect that you would go on to make some effort to deal with the substantive matters to which my 'enormous effort' had addressed itself. Instead you mainly read me a lecture which seems to assume that the purpose of our dialogue is an exercise in good manners . . .

". . . I am saying that our 'enormous effort in commenting so carefully' on your draft deserved a response that would show some comparable effort and care on the part of the Quakers to understand, examine and weigh and measure the merits of our questions and arguments. Your letter makes no such showing despite your appreciated words of courtesy . . .

"You say that 'many' of my comments and criticism 'have been immensely thought-provoking.' Yet, as I have already mentioned, between the time you requested my comments and of your present letter to me, and presumably when my comments and those of Milton Konvitz were on your table, the step was taken of distributing your document among members of the Congress of the United States. It would be good to know what specific changes were made in the document as a result of my 'immensely thought-provoking' comments and criticisms. [Editor's Note: On this point, see letter of June 16, 1970, from Professor Stone to Professor Caplan, below.]

"You repeat in your letter the anticipatory defense, which I noticed in your Draft Ten also, that your group has no 'misguided belief that anyone is going to love you' because of your efforts to 'help some people to think about the Middle East for themselves.' But of course there is a great temptation, for one using this defense, to believe that the mere fact that one or both sides criticize him is itself warranty of conscientiousness and accuracy of his work.

"I was led to believe, indeed, that your committee's sole interest was to help the parties and the world in their search for a just and stable peace. Do you, for a moment, think that you can bring the parties closer to this objective unless the positions you take are ones which even if they cannot 'love' they can at any rate respect as representing the utmost conscientious effort to face truthfully the problems each party is really trying to grapple with?"

*From letter of April 13, 1970; Professor Boasson to Paul B. Johnson:*

". . . I would be insincere on my part if I were to say that your letter made me feel that I have been of any use or have contributed at all to improvements in your paper. The changes which you mention strike me as verbal only. . . . I feel, however, that some mere changes in the word-choice of your paper cannot alter its biased tenor. There has been some advantage even in blunt words which made the bias patent; more delicate formulation may now require more ample criticism. In short I do not believe that anything material of my criticisms has been taken account of seriously . . .

". . . As I pointed out, the paper ascribes to the Arab side positive peaceful attitudes which not always existed or were not at all representative, whilst ascribing to the Israel position negative aggressiveness and expansionism, which, if existing at all, were not necessarily representative. No wonder that your paper refrains from quoting the sources of the record which its authors (p. 9) purport to have been reading carefully.

"It also seems odd—whatever reasons are given for it—that of the side which is both most desirous and most in need of real peace, 'first steps' are more stringently required than of the original attackers (Trygve Lie, first Secretary General of the U.N., made no bones about that in his *Quest for Peace*) whilst these are still loudly professing their original aim, that of final liquidation."

*From letter of August 3, 1970; Professor Boasson to Hannah Newcombe, Canadian Peace Research Institute, and member of the Quaker Group:*

". . . Only last month I saw the February 1970 expanded (and even more shocking) version of the original Draft. We, at the Truman Center here, had a session with Landrum R. Bolling and Paul Johnson on some matters concerning the drafts. Our academic director, Julius Stone of Sydney University, and a visiting scholar, Milton Konvitz, pointed out some of the major defects which seemed to impress even your fellow draftsmen . . .

". . . After having compared the June 1969 and February 1970 versions I really experienced one of the most bitter disappointments in my never too rosy reliance on human capacities to be fair and reasonable. It is so intensely bitter for two reasons: I knew some of the efforts of the Quakers to contribute to what Francis Bacon called 'the relief of man's estate' and if the Quakers are an 'elite' in this respect, what is to be expected from others? The second reason is that I now saw the growth of the document not simply resulting from the naive and insufficient information but as it were arrived at *parti pris* from the beginning and later supplemented with deliberate distortions of which no charitable explanation is possible any longer."

*From letter of June 16, 1970; Professor Stone to Professor Gerald Caplan of Harvard University:*

"It may be very relevant to know that when I saw Paul Johnson at the Truman Building opening, I pressed him hard about their circulation of the Quaker document in mimeograph among Congressmen at the time of the last decision about the Phantoms.

"He claimed that the circulation was by a Washington, D. C. branch without the group's knowledge.

"I pressed him as to whether that circulated draft was different from what they were about to publish. He said, yes, substantially different.

"I then asked whether the group did not have a duty to write to each Congressman immediately and inform him that circulation has been improperly made, and that the document circulated did not in a number of respects represent their position.

"He was (it seemed to me) quite shameless in saying that, no, they had no such duty. After putting the same question to him three ways, I decided that the fault was not in his good understanding, but in his good intentions."

The experience of Professors Stone, Konvitz and Boasson with the Quaker group, as indicated by the letters cited above, would seem to raise some important points, among them the following:

(1) From Dr. Bolling's own admission, reported by Professor Stone, the Quakers received "U.S. governmental suggestions that a pro-Arab slant is required," and Dr. Bolling, the editor of the Quaker report, "tended to agree" with those suggestions. Was the Quaker report, therefore, designed and edited to produce a "pro-Arab slant?" If so, should its pretensions to objectivity and neutrality be dismissed as a mere sham?

(2) Where did the "U.S. governmental suggestions" originate? Could they have come from the chronically pro-Arab old Middle East hands of the State Department? Were there also other suggestions that tied the final Quaker proposals to the so-called "Rogers Plan?"

(3) Were the doubts of the Jewish scholars as to the good faith of the Quaker group—doubts which developed out of their

experience in discussing the various drafts—justified? Did the Quakers use their meetings with Jewish experts as part of a serious effort to develop additional insight, knowledge and sound analysis? Or were these meetings merely a means of supporting their public claim to have "listened to all sides" and to get an early warning on points of exceptional sensitivity where verbal cosmetics could soften and make future criticism more difficult?

(4) It is a fact that a preliminary draft of the Quaker report was distributed to members of the U.S. Congress in the spring of 1970. Was it mere coincidence that this distribution was made just when the sale of Phantom aircraft to Israel was under consideration?

(5) Paul Johnson claimed that the draft had been circulated by a Washington, D. C. branch without the group's knowledge. Was it not Frances Neely, the Friends' chief lobbyist in Washington and herself a member of the Quaker study group, who arranged its circulation to members of the U.S. Congress at that critical time?

## CHAPTER II

# THE RISE OF THE STATE OF ISRAEL

Repeated references in the Quaker report uncritically accept the Arab argument that Israel was imposed on the area by Western states guilty of anti-Semitism to solve, at Arab expense, a problem Arabs never created. This Arab propaganda claim is false in all its parts. Nevertheless, the Quaker report furthers the Arab line. The following quotation is one example:

> "At partition, the Palestinian Arabs saw themselves being forced to give up much of their lands, private and communal, to Jewish settlers as part of a grand-scale international effort at restitution and compensation to the Jews. The Palestinian Arabs, chiefly a Muslim people, concluded that they were being required to pay for the anti-Semitic sins of the Christian West." (p. 24)

Here the Quaker authors clearly identify this argument as representing the Arab position. But the report gradually adopts the Arab line as its own without even a pretense of critical inquiry into the historical or logical grounds on which the Arab argument is based.

> "The great powers . . . share the guilt for perpetuating anti-Semitism into the era of the multi-religious, secular state. They helped to create the conditions which stimulated the longing of many Jews for the presumed safety of a national home." (p. 54)

> ". . . anti-Jewish prejudices, discrimination and persecution are not a problem which the Arab countries must be expected to solve for the rest of the world by repeatedly trading away Arab territory. To place that burden upon the Arabs is to transfer from the West to the Middle East the most loathsome aspects of the anti-Jewish madness and to make peace for the area, in any true sense, impossible." (p. 94)

Here, in strident form, is the straight Arab propaganda line, advanced as a conclusion of the authors. Any objective review of the relevant history shows this to be false and misleading. (For a brief study of land ownership in Palestine 1880-1948, see Appendix I.)

Without exonerating Western nations of anti-Semitism or guilt towards Jews, one must recognize that Jews have not fled from the United States or Western Europe for safety in Israel. If anyone has a relatively clean record on the treatment of the Jews, it is these Western countries. In the exceptional case of Hitler's Germany, for most of those trapped by Nazism flight was impossible. A remnant of Jews who did manage to escape death in the Holocaust were absorbed into the dynamic and determined movement for freedom which had long characterized the Jewish community of Palestine.

Arab and Moslem countries may claim a relative humaneness in their dealings with Jews *only* by comparison with Hitler's Germany but they are in no position to deny responsibility for the Jewish problem.

The Quaker report exemplifies the purported "enlightened policies Islamic rulers followed" (pp. 13-14), by reference to Maimonides, the most famous of the medieval Jewish leaders, who attained an exalted position as court physician to Saladin the Great. They fail to mention that Maimonides fled to Egypt not from Christian persecution but from Moslem fanatics in Spain. He was later forced to hide his Judaism in order to preserve his security among the Moslems of Africa and Arabia. He is famous for his letter advising Yemenite Jews how to cope with their enforced conversion to Islam.

Moreover, before the rise of modern Zionism, the major problems of persecution and expulsion of Jews during the 19th Century arose in Morocco, Algeria and Persia; in the 1870's, when Rumania was still part, however autonomous, of the Ottoman Empire, the oppression was so great that total evacuation of the Jews was considered by Jewish organizations.

More than half the Jewish population of Israel today comes from Moslem countries. Unlike the Arabs, who left large communities behind in Israel consisting of those who chose *not* to flee, the exodus of Jews from Iraq, Yemen, Syria, Libya, Tunisia, Egypt and other Moslem countries had been almost complete.

The Quaker report completely ignores this fact and its implications. Instead, after a substantial section on the plight of the Arab refugees, it barely mentions that expelled Jews also deserve to be considered in solving the refugee problem. The Quakers then hasten to explain, however, that many Jews emigrated voluntarily or were recruited; such Jews should therefore be omitted from any calculation for compensation claims. (p. 101)

Nowhere does the report propose to examine how many Arabs left Israel voluntarily or were recruited or advised by Arabs and helped by the British to leave; nor does it suggest that this number should be deducted from the total number of Arab refugees to be compensated. (pp. 38-42)

Israel arose as the necessary and only constructive permanent solution for the Jewish problem in Eastern Europe, and for the Jewish victims of persecution and/or expulsion in Moslem lands. Israel's present population mix—less than half from Europe, and more than half from Arab countries—reflects the conditions that brought it into being. To omit or overlook the persecution of Jews living in the Middle East as a primary factor in the creation of the Jewish state is to turn one's back on history.

Further, it is historical nonsense to say that Western states created Israel, or "imposed" it on the Arabs. (See p. 85) The Quaker report not only records this Arab propaganda line without modification or quotation marks but gives a false historical account of Israel's rise.

The Balfour Declaration of 1917 was a wartime effort to win Jewish support for the allies in the U.S. and Russia and to overcome pro-German sympathies arising out of hatred for the Czar. After the war, the Balfour Declaration was included in the League of Nations' Mandate in order to give Britain an acceptable justification for what it intended to do anyway—exclude France from the Holy Land. When the war was over Jewish support was no longer needed by the British.

British policy had long sought control over a solid Arab bloc. Having done nothing to advance Zionism after about 1922 (when the Mandate was approved), London decided in the 1930's to freeze Zionist development. The 1939 White Paper barring further Jewish immigration to Palestine was the culmination of this policy; it also served as the death warrant for hundreds of thousands of Jews trapped inside Nazi Europe. Under pressure of Arab revolts and Axis propaganda—and at the expense of Jewish lives—London sought to construct an Arab Palestine as part of a British-dominated *Arab* bloc.

This policy was still in effect when World War II ended, blighting the hopes of Jewish survivors of Nazism who were forced to seek illegal entry into Palestine—and nourishing the growth of Jewish militancy. Britain had no alternative but to forcibly repress the Jewish community or to give up the Mandate.

In 1947 a study by the United Nations Special Committee on Palestine (UNSCOP), representing Australia, Canada, Czechoslovakia, Guatemala, India, Iran, the Netherlands, Peru, Sweden, Uruguay and Yugoslavia, recommended the partition of Palestine into a Jewish and an Arab state. The UNSCOP report was adopted by the U.N., with more than the necessary two-thirds vote. The U.S.S.R. strongly supported the partition plan as the best way to get Britain out of Palestine. American support, which was given because no other solution seemed possible, was reluctant. Great Britain abstained from voting. The Jews accepted the plan. The Arabs rejected it.

The basis for the partition was the undeniable fact (not mentioned in the Quaker report any more than the rest of this history) that the Jewish community in Palestine (known as the Yishuv) was too determined on independence for any other proposal to be workable. American agreement to the partition, reluctant throughout, was based on hope that Britain would help implement it.

Instead, Britain blocked any implementation of the U.N. plan, still cherishing the strategic dream of a British-aligned Arab bloc and hoping that the sabotage of the U.N. proposal by the Arabs would further British ends. Under strong British influence, America backed down; on March 19, 1948 the U.S. representative in the U.N. Security Council, Warren Austin, announced a reversal of U.S. policy. The U.S. proposed that the partition plan be suspended and that a special session of the General Assembly be called in order to approve a U.N. trusteeship for Palestine instead. Despite efforts by the U.S., France and others, however, the General Assembly did not rescind the partition resolution. Britain announced it would abandon the Mandate and withdraw its troops from Palestine and on May 14 the State of Israel was established. President Truman quickly accepted the *fait accompli* and recognized the new state. Israel was therefore neither created by nor imposed by the West, but arose in spite of obstruction, opposition, or inactivity by most of the great Western powers. Israel was created by Jews who had settled the land, turned desert and swamp into garden and grove, and who now demanded sovereignty for themselves and for their fellow-Jews in Europe and

Moslem lands seeking security and dignity in the historic homeland of the Jewish people.

The Quaker report's account of Israel's creation, by repeating without question or quotation marks the Arab propaganda version that it was imposed from the outside, is more than an instance of the moral masochism so often found in Western democracies: the wish to bear symbolic crosses for uncommitted sins. Considering the total omission of the main facts of this history, the report can only be regarded as a work of deliberate distortion.

The report functions, in this case, to bolster the Arabs' claim that Israel's very existence is an injustice against them because they had no share in the Jewish problem. This is as false as is the parallel contention, reported with silent assent, that the great powers, having imposed Israel on the Arabs, must now make amends. An impartial factual report would not have omitted the history of Israel's painful development, which flatly contradicts Arab pretensions.

## CHAPTER III

# THE WAR OF INDEPENDENCE, 1948

The Quaker account of the 1948 fighting is grossly distorted. For example, Britain's important role in turning over key installations and equipment to the Arabs is not mentioned. The report falsely implies that the conflict erupted spontaneously and simultaneously on both sides. In fact the conflict was launched by the Arabs despite Jewish appeals for peace and co-existence. The Arabs not merely "never accepted" (as the Quakers gently put it), the U.N. partition of Palestine, but attempted to destroy it by force of arms before it could be implemented. This is how the report equates Israel's efforts to create a state and Arab efforts to destroy it:

> "Long before the partition plan could go into effect, however, clashes developed between underground groups and para-military units already active on both sides." (p. 25)

The Jewish effort to save their prospective state—as well as their homes and lives—is not mentioned except in the context of strategically pointless "terror and counter-terror." Nor does the report consider it relevant to mention that the original partition plan was based on the assumption that no defense of borders would be necessary. The lines drawn reflected mainly the concentrations of population: where Arabs predominated, the territory was included in the Palestinian state to be; where Jews were in the majority—on the coastal plain and in parts of the Galilee, for example—the territory was incorporated into the projected Jewish state. Thus, although the Friends' study repeats and ultimately accepts the myth that partition forced the Palestinian Arabs "to give up much of their lands, private and communal, to Jewish settlers as part of a grand-scale international effort at restitution and compensation to the Jews," the fact is that the U.N. partition plans of 1947 did not call upon anyone to give up any land.

In view of the assumption of peaceful co-existence between the new Arab and the new Jewish state, there was no necessity for any private lands or governmental lands to be given up or exchanged. But the partition plan could have been viable only if Arabs and Jews peacefully accepted it and continued to live peacefully within its provisions. Instead, the surrounding Arab states invaded Israel, plunging the Middle East into war, only to be driven back.

The Arabs' rejection of the U.N. plan and their armed attack not only destroyed the hope for the peaceful partition of Palestine but made a new map essential to any peaceful solution, a map with new and defensible frontiers. An armistice was achieved in negotiations between the parties under U.N. sponsorship only after the Security Council called on the parties to disengage their forces along new demarcation lines—continuous, more defensible and secure, and less irrational.

None of this appears in the report, which contents itself with noting that Israel now controlled lands beyond the original partition. What *is* mentioned provides the psychological atmosphere for insinuations of Israeli aggression and aims for territorial aggrandizement.

Arab aggression is not mentioned. Nor is the fact that a lasting truce could only arise when more secure frontiers were negotiated and agreed to by the parties. Thus does the report prepare the reader implicitly to convert Israel into the aggressor in subsequent encounters and to disregard the critical importance of secure and agreed boundaries as a precondition for any lasting peace.

## CHAPTER IV

# THE QUAKER REPORT ON THE WAR OF 1956

In the authors' treatment of the 1956 war, again crucial facts are ignored and those employed distorted. The report charges that as a result of the international crisis precipitated by Nasser's nationalization of the Suez Canal in 1956, "the Israelis saw an opportunity to settle accumulated scores with Egypt." It mentions sundry other objectives and refers, with total obscurity, to "a debate which had raged inside the Israeli cabinet for many months [and which] was resolved in favor of the hard line faction. . . ."

What the issues debated in the Cabinet were the report fails to mention: the Arab blockade at Sharm el Sheikh; the illegal closure of the Suez Canal; the formation of a ring of Arab foes in military alliance around Israel; and the rapidly changing balance of military power flowing from the Soviet-Egyptian arms deal. The Quaker authors mention only the "recurring border attacks by terrorists organized and directed by Egypt." (Between 1948 and 1956, 1,500 Israeli citizens were killed by Arab terrorists. Viewed in terms of U.S. population, this figure would be the equivalent of 20,000 Americans killed per year.)

The Jewish state was not the main immediate target of Egyptian strategic aims, although unremitting and (with new Soviet military and diplomatic support) increasingly ruthless and bloody pressure was exerted against Israel. Nasser had bigger fish to fry. After the election of President Eisenhower in 1952, the main concern of Arab leaders centered on the implications of Secretary Dulles' plans to build up a Middle East defensive deterrent alliance against the Russians. In American as in earlier British strategy, the hope of a solid Arab front was a main consideration. Against this, Israeli interests had little weight. But any such plan ran into the internecine Arab struggle between Egypt and Iraq.

While Egypt continued to bargain, Secretary Dulles proceeded with his "northern tier" approach through Iraq. On January 12, 1955, the world was informed of the prospective Turkish-Iraqi military security pact (concluded on February 24, 1955), out of which grew the Baghdad Pact. This treaty, coming well before Secretary Dulles' refusal to finance the Aswan Dam, was the primary reason for Nasser's turn to the U.S.S.R. It was during this period (not months later in response to Israel's February 28 Gaza raid, nor at the Bandung conference in April, nor following arms negotiations with Washington that continued until June) that Nasser took up a long-standing option to accept military aid from the Soviet Union (via Czechoslovakia) in such quantity and of such advanced type as to upset entirely the military and political balance in the area.

The 1955 Soviet-Egyptian arms deal is never mentioned in the Quaker report's sketch of the background of the 1956 war. (There is a reference to Soviet arms supplies for Arab states, in a section on "Soviet Views on Peace in the Middle East," which omits any facts that would show Soviet contributions to the promotion of military crises in the Middle East. The report simply conveys without quotation marks official Soviet versions of the issues.) Nor does the report show any awareness of the Tripartite Agreement or any other arrangement of the Western powers or of the U.N. for damping down military confrontations between 1948 and 1956.

The report's basic assumption—submitted without factual evidence—emerges from the following casual statement referring to the period after 1948:

> "The Arabs had been beaten and humiliated, but neither the Israelis nor the United Nations could compel them to make peace."

The implication is that having imposed Israel on the Arabs, the U.N. then tried to "compel them to make peace."

This misrepresentation is not a trifling issue. The insinuation that the U.N. sincerely tried and failed to compel Arabs to make peace is necessary to one of the report's primary conclusions: that experience has proved the parties directly involved incapable of negotiating peace themselves.

The fact is that from the outset, the role of the U.N. and of the Western powers was not to compel Arabs to make peace but to make it unnecessary for them to do so. The only significant departure from this role was when the 1949 armistice was finally negotiated by Ralph Bunche, and then it was because he operated under a Security Council resolution that ordered the parties to negotiate and regroup their forces behind mutually agreed viable truce demarcation lines as a first step toward peace.

The U.N. Conciliation Commission (of U.S., French and Turkish composition) from its inception followed an opposite procedure. It began, during the armistice negotiations, by consulting the Arabs—but not the Israelis—on the procedures they would agree to follow. Later, having decided to try mediation, the Commission attempted to get an Arab commitment to peace as a first step. When this was rejected, the Commission agreed to proceed without it. Following the Conciliation Commission's failure, the U.N. General Assembly in 1952 defeated a resolution declaring the parties themselves directly responsible for negotiating a peace. This is where the idea began that peace negotiations between Arabs and Israel are not possible nor practical. It was repeated in similar U.N. acts thereafter. Given such a U.N. attitude, it is inevitable that Arabs opposed to Israel's existence should reject any need to negotiate. In the face of the Arab refusal, the Western Allies relied on a Tripartite Agreement to preserve the peace themselves. They also decided on a policy of a controlled arms supply to the Arabs and Israel aimed at maintaining a military balance in the Middle East. This balance, however, was totally disrupted by the 1955 Soviet-Egyptian arms deal, which immediately projected the conflict onto a new and far more deadly level of tank and jet aircraft combat.

This whole complex of pertinent facts is not mentioned in the report.

## CHAPTER V

# THE JUNE WAR OF 1967

The Quaker report details the 1967 war more fully than the 1948 and 1956 encounters. But the account contains positive distortions as well as negative omissions. It is an attempt to rewrite history to suit the authors' preconceived conclusions.

> "The authors of this paper, having studied the historical record and conferred with numerous experts on the Arab-Israeli conflict, accept the judgment that the war of June, 1967, was a war nobody intended to happen.
>
> "It is our conviction that the long accumulation of border incidents, of Palestinian Arab commando attacks and Israeli military reprisals had brought the area close to the point of explosion long before the U.A.R. called for a withdrawal of UN Emergency Forces from the Israeli-Sinai border and announced a blockade of the Strait of Tiran, that each side had made threats which the other side was bound to interpret as a prelude to an attack, and that the words and deeds of military leaders on each side carried each to a point of no return. We feel that the behavior of both the U.A.R. and Israel was provocative and precipitate. . . .
>
> "Finally, we are convinced that the Soviet Union and the United States did not always act responsibly over a period of two decades to 'cool' a situation which constituted an immense danger to the world." (pp. 36-37)

If the Six-Day War was about to explode "long before the U.A.R. called for a withdrawal of U.N. Emergency Forces from the Israeli-Sinai border and announced a blockade of the Strait of Tiran," nobody was aware of it at the time. Such a theory, allegedly based on "having studied the historical record," is not supported by any evidence whatever, nor is any offered. The report simply asserts that each side had reached "the point of no return" long before Nasser occupied Sharm el Sheikh. The fact is that Israel had made it crystal clear for ten years that such a move would constitute a *causus belli;* indeed once the Tiran Straits had been blockaded, Egypt boasted that Israel had no alternative but to resort to arms, as indicated in the following three quotations—none of which is cited in the Quaker report.

> "As of today, there no longer exists an international emergency force to protect Israel. . . . The sole method we shall apply against Israel is a total war which will result in the final extermination of Zionist existence." (*Voice of the Arabs Radio,* May 18, 1967)

> "Taking Sharm el Sheikh meant confrontation with Israel. Taking such action meant that we were ready to enter a general war with Israel." (President Nasser, May 22, 1967)

> "With the closing of the Gulf of Aqaba, Israel is faced with two alternatives, either of which will destroy it; it will either be strangled to death by the Arab military and economic blockade; or it will perish by the fire of the Arab forces encompassing it from the south, from the north and from the east." (Cairo Radio, May 30, 1967)

There were many more such pronouncements when Egypt expelled the U.N. Emergency Forces from the Sinai and Sharm el Sheikh. According to Field Marshal Amer's testimony in the March 1968 trials in Cairo, Nasser knew that these drastic steps would make war "almost certain."

Clearly, the decisive moves that precipitated the war of June 1967 were the unilateral actions of Nasser's Egypt. President Johnson recognized this fact in a statement on June 19, 1967:

> "If a single act of folly was more responsible for this explosion than any other, it was the arbitrary and dangerous announced decision that the Straits of Tiran would be closed."

The Quaker report makes no reference to this statement. On the contrary, it arbitrarily states that the area was "close to the point of explosion long before the U.A.R. called for a withdrawal of U.N. Emergency Forces." The report's omission of this and many other evidences of Arab responsibility for the Six-Day War leads the objective reader to the inevitable conclusion that the Quaker authors distorted the true history of the 1967 War in order to justify a set of predetermined conclusions that assigned equal blame for the outbreak of fighting to both sides. This even-handedness goes under the name of Quaker objectivity.

Perhaps the most glaring distortion in the report is its account of the U.S.S.R.'s notorious intelligence activity regarding Israel's alleged mobilization of the Syrian border in the spring of 1967. This story is told in such a way as to entirely camouflage Soviet responsibility for pushing the Arabs to the brink of war. From the Quaker "facts," no one could guess that the Russians, by design, brought Egypt into the war picture by publishing blatantly false reports about Israeli troop movements—reports which were actually designed to relieve internal strains and divisions in Syria that were threatening the future of Soviet influence in that state.

The facts, briefly, are these: in March 1967, Soviet Foreign Minister Gromyko advised Nasser to withdraw some troops from Yemen and deploy them in the Sinai peninsula in order to put military pressure on Israel's southern frontier. In May, the Syrians sent Nasser an alarming report (based on Soviet intelligence) that Israel had concentrated 19 brigades on their frontier. (Later, in his post-war speeches, Nasser said that he had checked and had established that there were indeed 13 brigades. In truth—as found by U.N. and other sources—there were none, and U Thant so reported to the U.N. on May 19, 1967. But Nasser insisted that he had moved his troops in order to discharge his duty to his Arab brothers.) Russian diplomats also "informed" Egypt that Israel was massing troops on the Syrian border. Soviet Ambassador Chuvakhin made a post-midnight call on Israel Prime Minister Eshkol to deliver Moscow's charge that Israel was concentrating troops near Syria. Eshkol three times invited the Soviet Ambassador to visit the area and see for himself, but Chuvakhin declined the invitation, stating that he was sure that Moscow knew what it was protesting about.

The Quakers report only part of the story and quickly add: "Both Russians and Arabs argued that in a small, heavily-armed country like Israel mobilization could be carried out overnight and there was no need for an advance build-up on the border." One wonders where that fable came from. There is nothing in the voluminous press reports or in official documentation to suggest that the Russians and the Arabs "argued" that Israel really didn't have to mobilize long in advance—unless they felt compelled to make that argument *after* U Thant's May 19th report to the U.N. demolished their charges of Israeli mobilization. The Quaker authors never mention this.

The fact is that Egypt, which had come to rely almost exclusively on Soviet intelligence about Israel, was deliberately misled by the Russians into accepting the argument that only a massive Egyptian mobilization in the Sinai could save Damascus. The Egyptian War Minister, Badran, later testified at his trial in Cairo that the Egyptians had discovered too late that the Soviet "information" had been a "mere hallucination." It is now clear that the Russians intended to repeat their oft-used stratagem of manufacturing a false "invasion danger" and then to pose as the "saviors" of the Syrian regime. With the U.N. Expeditionary Force as a buffer between Egypt and Israel, especially at Sharm el Sheikh, the Soviets felt confident that war would not occur. But Nasser demanded that the U.N. presence be withdrawn and U Thant complied at once, ordering the U.N. Emergency Force to leave immediately and entirely, despite the provisions for delaying precisely such a contingency detailed in the Hammarskjold memorandum. Only then was the area brought "to the point of explosion."

The Quaker account of these crucial days is slanted to support the Egyptians' post-war propaganda claim that they were massing troops in forward positions in Sinai and Sharm el Sheikh, and making radio and television threats of genocide, merely to defend themselves against Israeli aggression. The Quaker report declares with a straight face that "The Arabs . . . including specifically President Nasser insist that they did not intend to attack Israel but had only tried to get themselves in readiness to meet the Israeli blow, which in fact did come." (p. 35)

This clear and conscious distortion of history provides the "factual" basis for the report's conclusions on two crucial points. The first is ". . . that the behavior of both the U.A.R. and Israel was provocative and precipitate"—meaning that both sides were equally guilty for the outbreak of war in 1967. Such a judgment is preposterous. The record of events and proceedings in the United Nations prior to June 5, 1967 and the public record in the world's news media proves otherwise. If both sides were equally provocative, what Israeli provocations were comparable to Egypt's massive troop build-up in the Sinai, Egypt's demand for the removal of the U.N. peacekeeping forces, Egypt's occupation of Sharm el Sheikh, and Egypt's naval blockade against Israel? If both sides were equally precipitate, then the party that first commits an act of war (as the Straits of Tiran "blockade" had been clearly defined in international law) is no more responsible than the party that responds by force to that prior act of war.

The attaching of equal guilt for the Six-Day War to both sides was in itself a concession by the Quaker authors following criticism of an earlier draft of their report, which called the U.A.R. merely "inept" while charging Israel with being "aggressively irresponsible." But even in its final version the report manages to suggest that Egypt was innocent of any aggressive action or intention. For example, the report asserts that "Egyptian leaders had concluded that a massive build-up of Egyptian troops on the Israeli-Sinai frontier was needed to impress and deter the Israelis. . . . On May 16 the United Nations was requested to withdraw its Emergency Forces. . . so that U.A.R. troops could move up to the border, as General Fawzi, Egyptian Chief of Staff, put it, 'to be ready for action against Israel the moment it might carry out an aggressive action against any Arab country.' " (p. 34) Moreover, "President Nasser and other Egyptian officials have said that they never intended for the U.N.E.F. to withdraw completely from the Sinai and certainly not from Sharm el Sheikh. . ." (p. 35)

The disingenuous if not curious nature of these *ex post facto*, self-serving statements—particularly in view of the militant and determined actions the Egyptians took in May, 1967 (the U.N.E.F., for example, was literally forced out by Egyptian troops moving up to the border)—somehow escapes the critical faculties of the Quaker authors. Instead, they accept at face value Nasser's postwar excuse that he did not really intend to attack Israel. The conclusion is inevitable if unstated: Israel was the aggressor in 1967; its purpose—to acquire territory. In any peace settlement, therefore, the principle of non-acquisition of territory must apply. The possibility that Israel acted in self-defense, not in pursuit of territorial expansion, is simply ignored. Therefore, there can be no question of applying the principle of secure and agreed boundaries (as opposed to the kind of boundaries that encouraged the 1967 Arab aggression) in any peace settlement recommended by the authors of *Search for Peace in the Middle East*.

The report also relieves the Soviet Union of any responsibility for the fabrications that had such direct influence in plunging the Middle East into war and the Arabs into catastrophe. This makes it possible for the authors to treat the United States and the Soviet Union in the same even-handed manner that assigns equal responsibility to Israel and the Arabs for the outbreak of fighting.

"We are convinced," the report declares, "that the Soviet Union and the United States did not always act responsibly over a period of two decades to 'cool' a situation which constituted an immense danger to the world." (p. 37)

And later:

"It is the judgment of the authors of this paper that a large measure of responsibility for the distressing continuance of conflict in the Middle East rests upon the great powers, both historically and at present." (p. 67)

This display of even-handedness is not a casual good will gesture. It is essential to the Quakers' repeated calls for Big Power, Big Four, U.S.-U.S.S.R. or Security Council action as a substitute for direct negotiations between the Arab states and Israel. It is also vital to the report's thesis that third party security "guarantees" are more important than a true, final and binding peace treaty signed by the states concerned. The fact remains, however, that the U.S.S.R.'s active and pernicious intervention in the spring of 1967 paved the way to war. The U.S. cannot be charged with any similar intercession. Yet the authors of the Quaker report persist in the assumption that objectivity is achieved not by considering all the facts but by blaming all the parties. A full and thorough review of Soviet Russia's actions in the 1967 crisis would in fact reveal most of the report's "Suggestions for the Bases of a Practical Peace Settlement" to be naive, dangerous and absurd.

Indeed, there are so many distortions and omissions in this section of the Quaker report that there is not enough space in this book to take up all of them. But two more major points do deserve attention.

> "U Thant's action brought about total U.N.E.F. withdrawal including the handing over of Sharm el Sheikh to the U.A.R. military control. Once the U.A.R. authorities were installed there again, they felt bound to re-institute the blockade of Israeli shipping in the Strait of Tiran which they had been forced to give up as the result of the Israeli attack in 1956 and the Israeli withdrawal 'deal' worked out by the Americans." (p. 35)

The report never does explain why the U.A.R. "felt bound to re-institute the blockade of Israeli shipping." Nor does it mention Nasser's bellicose statements at the time:

> "Our basic objective will be the destruction of Israel. The Arab people want to fight.

"The meaning of Sharm el Sheikh is a confrontation with Israel. Adopting this measure obligates us to be ready to embark on a general war with Israel." (May 27)

"We will not accept any . . . coexistence with Israel. . . . Today the issue is not the establishment of peace between the Arab states and Israel." (May 28)

"The armies of Egypt, Jordan, Syria and Lebanon are poised on the borders of Israel . . . while standing behind us are the armies of Iraq, Algeria, Kuwait, Sudan and the whole Arab nation. This act will astound the world. Today they will know that the Arabs are arranged for battle. The critical hour has arrived. We have reached the stage of serious action and not of mere declarations." (May 30)

These are not the words of a leader who intends peace or who seeks merely to "impress and deter" his enemy. Even King Hussein of Jordan, in his book *My "War" with Israel* makes it clear that he knew the war became "inevitable" when Nasser closed Aqaba and massed troops in Sinai.

Even more significant, however, is the cavalier manner in which the Quaker authors speak of "the withdrawal 'deal' worked out by the Americans" after the 1956 war.

First, it may be recalled that Egypt had recognized the international character of the Straits of Tiran as far back as January 28, 1950, when it sent a note to the American Embassy in Cairo that said:

"It goes without saying that this passage [through the Strait of Tiran] will remain free as in the past in conformity with international practice and with the recognized principle of international law."

In 1957, 17 maritime powers declared at the U.N. that Israel had the right to transit the Straits. The Convention on the Territorial Sea and Contiguous Zone adopted by the U.N. Conference on the Law of the Sea, adopted April 27, 1958, and effective from September 10, 1964, stipulated:

"There shall be no suspension of the innocent passage of foreign ships through straits which are used for international navigation between one part of the high seas and another part of the high seas or the territorial sea of a foreign state."

This stipulation was made because of the history of problems arising from Egypt's action in 1951, when despite her pledge one year earlier she closed the Straits to Israeli shipping.

With the international character of the Straits clearly in mind, and with actions to further clarify the issue in prospect at the U.N. and elsewhere, the United States undertook to guarantee freedom of passage for Israel through the Straits in 1957; Great Britain, France and other maritime powers joined in that guarantee. The U.S. and the U.N., with Soviet agreement, also guaranteed that Egyptian armed forces would not return to the Gaza Strip. The United Nations Emergency Force was established as the tangible expression of these undertakings, and only after the U.N.E.F. was physically present at Sharm el Sheikh and along the Egyptian side of the Sinai frontier did the Israeli troops withdraw.

Clearly, the "withdrawal 'deal' worked out by the Americans" included serious commitments from other member states of the United Nations and from the U.N. itself. It was only on the basis of these international commitments that Israel agreed to withdraw. The U.N. record is full of corroborative testimony to the effect that all the terms and conditions were carefully scrutinized, clarified and solemnly adopted. The fact that none of the "guarantees" and "undertakings" by the U.N. and the powers were honored when Egypt imposed a state of war on the area is hardly evidence that there was no clear, unambiguous and legally binding agreement. The fact is that there was no "deal"; the snide reference in the Quaker report is a blatant effort to downgrade the importance of the big power guarantees, solemn international undertakings, and U.N. peace-keeping forces that failed to preserve peace in the Middle East. Since the report's own recommendations call for essentially the same "solution" to the post-1967 Arab-Israeli situation, it is little wonder that the authors seek to diminish the significance of the earlier failure.

Finally, the Quaker report's treatment of the role of Jordan in the war of 1967 merits analysis. In the whole section entitled "The Escalating Crisis," which purports to establish the background of the 1967 war, there is not a single word about the role of Jordan. The fact that, on May 30, 1967, King Hussein flew to Cairo, kissed President Nasser in front of world television cameras and signed a five-year mutual defense pact with Egypt is ignored. The fact that this treaty called for a joint defense council and a joint command with the chief-of-staff of the U.A.R. armed forces to "take over the command of such operations in both countries" is disregarded. Also omitted from the report is this item from the May 31, 1967 issue of the authoritative Cairo daily *Al Akhbar:*

> "Under terms of the military agreement signed with Jordan, Jordanian artillery coordinated with the forces of Egypt and Syria is in a position to cut Israel in two at Kalkilya, where Israeli territory between the Jordan armistice line and the Mediterranean Sea is only 12 kilometers wide. . . ."

Similarly absent from the Quaker report is this excerpt from the June 2 issue of the newspaper *Al Hayat* in which Hussein stated:

> "Our increased cooperation with Egypt and other Arab states both in the east and in the west will enable us to march along the right road which will lead us to the erasure of the shame and the liberation of Palestine."

The reader of the Quaker report would not know that Egyptian forces moved into Jordan and the Egyptian General Abdul Moneim Riyad took command. He would not be aware that American Patton tanks, supplied to Jordan by the United States, were stationed on the West Bank to be used against Israel. There is no reference to the statement in Hussein's book, *My "War" With Israel,* that in the days just prior to June 5, both Egypt and Jordan were awaiting only troop and aerial support from Iraq, Saudi Arabia and Syria before launching their attack against Israel.

Not mentioned in the Quaker report is that on June 5, when Israel moved against Egypt, it did not move against Jordan and that it sent the following message to Hussein:

> "We shall not initiate any action whatsoever against Jordan. However, should Jordan open hostilities, we shall react with all our might and he [King Hussein] will have to bear the full responsibility for all the consequences."

Although this effort by Israel to prevent war with Jordan has been confirmed by General Odd Bull, chief of the U.N. truce forces in the area, it is not discussed in the report, nor is the fact that Jordan responded with the bombardment of Jerusalem from Nebi Samuel and other high points around the Holy City and the seizure of Government House, the U.N. headquarters. Nor is there any hint in the Quaker report that at 9:15 a.m. on June 5, Radio Amman told its listeners:

> "The hoped for moment has arrived. The hour which you longed for is here. Forward to arms, to battle, to new pages of glory."

Again, the conclusion appears inescapable that the authors of the Quaker report suppressed the facts concerning Jordan's role in "The Escalating Crisis" because these facts effectively contradict the insinuation that Israel moved "aggressively" in quest of territorial expansion. Indeed, given Jordan's actual performance up to and including June 5, 1967, the importance to the future of peace in the area of "secure and agreed" boundaries is manifest. The report's call for a return to the insecure pre-June 1967 frontiers loses its moral and strategic foundations once the true facts of the 1967 war are admitted.

## CHAPTER VI

# THE U.N. RESOLUTION OF NOVEMBER 22, 1967

Throughout the Quaker report there are numerous citations of the November 22, 1967 Resolution of the Security Council (Resolution 242) "which spelled out the basic guidelines for a comprehensive Middle East peace." But the emphasis and intent of that Resolution are distorted when the authors assert that it "has been the starting point for the Big Four Talks." (p. 52)

While the U.N. Resolution is not unambiguous, it neither states nor implies that any other powers should intrude on the efforts of the U.N.'s special representative, Ambassador Gunnar Jarring, "to establish and maintain contacts with the states concerned in order to promote agreement and assist efforts to achieve a peaceful and accepted settlement in accordance with the provisions and principles of this resolution."

The basic concept of Big Four talks and the implications of Big Four pressures have excited much discussion in the U.S. and elsewhere, but it is misleading to infer that such talks somehow flow from the U.N. Resolution. A much stronger case can be made that Big Four talks detract from the responsibilities the Resolution charges to the U.N. representative since they involve parties other than "the states concerned." But there are more significant aspects of the Quaker report's interpretation of that Resolution which must concern us.

First, the Quaker authors "are persuaded that . . . the Soviet leaders have a genuine desire to see a political settlement along the lines of U.N. Resolution 242." But they avoid any clear recognition of the crucial differences of interpretation that have arisen with respect to Resolution 242.

According to the report, the Russians and Arabs interpret the Resolution as one that "requires a withdrawal of Israeli forces from all territories occupied after June 5, 1967 but does not require the Arab states to carry on direct negotiations with Israel." (p. 62) In fact, the consistent Arab position, fully supported by the U.S.S.R., is that complete Israeli withdrawal from all occupied territories must precede any negotiations.

The Russian and Arab view also interprets the Resolution to be self-executing—that is, that Israeli withdrawal is automatically called for and need not be the subject of negotiation. Hence, the argument of the U.S.S.R. that Big Four pressure is justified in order to force Israel to comply with that "requirement" of the Resolution.

The view of the United States and Israel on these points, as on others, has been quite different. First, the precise wording of the Resolution, which was unanimously adopted, was in the English language and reads "withdrawal of Israeli armed forces from territories"—not withdrawal from *the* territories or from *all the* territories. Lord Caradon, the British Ambassador to the U.N., who presented the final draft for acceptance by the Security Council, firmly and openly rejected pressures from Arab and other states to adopt their alternative formulation—namely, that the resolution require Israeli withdrawal from "all the territories." Lord Caradon also refused to accept the Indian delegate's argument, supported by the threat of a Soviet veto, that the Indian understanding of the resolution embodied the definite article *the* before "territories." It was made plain in the U.N. that the resolution "said what it said and did not say what it did not say." Thus, "withdrawal of Israeli armed forces from territories"—the language adopted without modification—does not specify precisely which territories, nor does it imply a timetable for any withdrawal.

In the U.S. and Israeli view, the U.N. resolution is not self-executing but requires negotiations which will lead to "agreement between the parties and among the parties." (See Secretary of State William Rogers' statement of March 27, 1969, below.) Also, since the resolution includes a series of inter-connected and interdependent principles, it calls on the U.N. representative "to promote agreement" between the opposing sides. The resolution cannot be interpreted to compel one side (Israel) to carry out one of the provisions (that concerning withdrawal) without agreement having been reached on the total package. Moreover, the resolution specifically calls for the right of every state in the area "to live in peace within secure and recognized boundaries free from threats or acts of force." Clearly such boundaries must be negotiated by the parties themselves: there is no ground for imposing a settlement through Big Four or other outside pressures.

This interpretation of Resolution 242 was embodied in a long series of statements by official American spokesmen. U.S. Ambassador to the United Nations Arthur Goldberg, who played a key role in the drafting and final passage of the resolution, said on May 15, 1969:

> "The premises underlying our support for the Resolution were these: What the Middle East needs is a real, just and lasting peace, acceptable and agreed upon by the parties. . . . Something more than the fragile much violated armistice that prevailed for 19 years. As we said (and it is an important premise), to return to the situation as it was before the 1967 war is not a prescription for peace but for renewed hostilities . . .
>
> "Withdrawal of Israeli troops, we held, should be in the context of and pursuant to a peace settlement accepted and agreed upon between the parties. Such a settlement will necessarily entail agreement on secure and recognized boundaries, ensuring the right of both Israel and her Arab neighbors to live in peace, free from threats or acts of force.
>
> "The Resolution of November 22, 1967, in its first operative paragraph, explicitly treats at the same time with both of these vital necessities of peace: on one hand, the withdrawal of Israeli forces; on the other hand, termination of the Arab's claims of belligerency, together with respect for, and acknowledgement of, Israel's sovereignty and her right to live in peace within secure and recognized boundaries. . . . History shows that if boundaries are to be secure, they cannot be determined unilaterally or imposed from the outside; they must be worked out by the parties themselves in the process of making peace . . .
>
> "Finally, it was a clear premise of the U.S. vote on the November 22 Resolution that the parties to the conflict must be parties to the peace. It is they who, sooner or later, must make a settlement. . . . Other countries can help; but the time when even great nations could impose their will on small ones is long past.
>
> "These were the premises—even-handed premises, in my opinion—that underlay our Government's support of the resolution.
>
> "Fundamentally, the Resolution is not self-executing, nor can it be implemented by unilateral action. It states general principles and envisions 'agreement' on specifics; the parties must put flesh on these bare bones.
>
> "If . . . the four powers, either singly or in combination, seek to impose a settlement on the parties, then I fear their efforts will fail.
>
> "No good can come from any attempt to impose a settlement. On

the contrary, much mischief may result from such an enterprise. This is the lesson of the last 20 years, particularly of the Suez crisis in 1956-57, when our country took the lead in imposing a settlement. We were singularly unsuccessful in achieving the just and permanent peace we sought; and even the makeshift arrangements of 1957 fell apart in May 1967."

*President Lyndon Johnson in a major address on the Middle East, September 10, 1968:*

"We are not the ones to say where other nations should draw lines between them that will assure each the greatest security. It is clear, however, that a return to the situation of June 4, 1967, will not bring peace. There must be secure and recognized borders. Some such lines must be agreed to by the neighbors involved as part of the transition from armistice to peace. At the same time, it should be clear that boundaries cannot and should not reflect the weight of conquest. Each side must have a reason, which each side, in honest negotiation, can accept as part of a just compromise."

*President Richard Nixon in a statement March 4, 1969:*

"The Four Powers . . . cannot dictate a settlement in the Middle East. The time has passed in which great nations can dictate to small nations their future where their vital interests are involved."

*Secretary of State William Rogers in a statement before the Senate Foreign Relations Committee, March 27, 1969:*

"[Jarring's] mission is to promote agreement—and this can only mean agreement between the parties and among the parties. We lay stress on this point because we do not believe that a peace settlement to which the parties did not agree could be just or lasting or, for that matter, attainable at all. We, for our part, are not interested in imposing a peace."

These and other expositions of the American view on Resolution 242 clearly emphasized the need for meaningful negotiations among the parties to the conflict. The operative meaning of the U.S. position was equally clear: since the resolution called for "secure and recognized" borders, there could be no return to the prewar lines of June 4, 1967, which obviously could not be described as "secure" because history had proved that they were not. On the other hand, if the borders were to be "recognized" by the Arabs, they could not be identical with the new cease-fire lines of June 10, 1967, which reflected the "weight of conquest." The previously cited U.S. position was that the parties to the conflict would arrive through negotiation at borders that would be identical with neither the lines of June 4 nor those of June 10, 1967, but somewhere in between. Each frontier segment would be determined by the parties on the basis of a solid "reason"—presumably of a security nature.

But this clear exposition of the American view somehow escaped the attention of the Quaker authors. Instead, they adopted the Russian-Arab view that negotiations among the parties are not the prerequisite for a durable peace and that Big Power intervention offers the best chance for a settlement. "It does not seem likely that the super-powers can 'impose' peace," say the Quakers in a bow to the oft-repeated rejection of such a course by the U.S. But they add in their conclusions: "The two super-powers have particular responsibilities to press for the speedy implementation of U.N. Resolution 242, in its entirety, as the way to peace." (p. 67)

Note that the key word "impose" is put in quotes, as if to signal the need to impose a settlement by more subtle means than sheer force. Surely, "speedy implementation" without full and free prior agreement by the parties concerned can only be in accordance with the Russian-Arab interpretation. In this connection, the Quaker report fails to mention that the Resolution refers explicitly to Article 2 of the U.N. Charter, which calls on all members to recognize the territorial integrity and sovereignty of all other members, to refrain from threats and acts of war, and to settle disputes peacefully. Despite the existence of Article 2, the authors seem to offer Israel recognition by the Arab states in exchange for a return to the pre-Six-Day War lines. While the resolution clearly does not say that Israel must withdraw from *all* the occupied territory, but should withdraw to negotiated "secure and recognized" boundaries, the Quaker authors start from the premise that the Soviet-Arab interpretation is correct and that while Israel is bound to withdraw from all the territories it occupied during the Six-Day War the Arabs are not required to carry on direct negotiations with Israel. This premise serves as the touchstone for all of the report's recommendations on how to achieve a Middle East peace.

It is not surprising, therefore, that the Quaker authors avoid mentioning prior statements of U.S. policy and restrict their description of the U.S. position to Secretary Rogers' speech of December 9, 1969. That speech marked a sharp retreat from the previously established American position. In an obvious desire to force some kind of settlement, the Secretary moved substantially in the direction of the Soviet-Arab position. And, in a complete about face, proposed what American policy had previously decried: predetermined boundary lines between Israel and Egypt and Israel and Jordan. With respect to Jordan, he called for nothing more than "insubstantial alterations" of the June 4, 1967 line. With respect to Egypt, he called for Israeli withdrawal to the old "international border." This essentially was a return to the borders of June 4, 1967.

Moreover, Mr. Rogers' December 9 speech, unlike earlier official U.S. pronouncements, omitted for the first time any declaration to the effect that America rejected the concept of an "imposed" settlement. On the contrary, the final paragraph of that speech included the following sentence: "We will not shrink from advocating necessary compromises, even though they may and probably will be unpalatable to both sides."

Yet, both before and since the launching of the "Rogers Plan," President Nixon has repeatedly stated with utmost clarity that the U.S. will not impose any settlement—indeed, that the U.S. will "maintain the arms balance."

If nothing else, an impartial, objective report would have been compelled to acknowledge the clear U.S. position established and maintained from June, 1967 to December, 1969—and reiterated, in fact, by President Nixon in a statement made on January 25, 1970, in which he said:

> "The United States believes that peace can be based only on agreement between the parties and that agreement can be achieved only through negotiations between them. We do not see any substitute for such negotiations if peace and security arrangements acceptable to the parties are to be worked out.
>
> "The United States does not intend to negotiate the terms of peace. It will not impose the terms of peace. We believe a durable peace agreement is one that is not one-sided and is one that all sides have a vested interest in maintaining. The United Nations resolution of November 1967 describes the principles of such a peace."

CHAPTER VII

# THE QUAKER REPORT ON THE PALESTINIANS

As one would expect, the Quaker report dwells at great length on the sufferings and frustrations of the Arab refugees. The American Friends Service Committee has done excellent humanitarian work on behalf of Arab refugees for more than 20 years. Empathy with the Arabs who suffered the consequences of three wars is consistent with the Quakers' best traditions as a group deeply concerned for humane values. But in the selection and interpretation of historical facts relevant to a clear and useful approach to the problems of the Palestinians, the report offers some curious examples of editorial distortion. This may be due to partisanship rooted in prolonged and close contact with the Palestinian refugees not only as a social and political problem but as human beings in need.

For example, despite repeated expressions supporting "the just recognition of claims denied to the abused Palestinian people," the Quaker report takes a rather one-sided approach to the history of that abuse. Any significant Arab responsibility for the plight of the Palestinian refugees is studiously avoided. There is no mention of the fact, recorded in United Nations documents, that it was Jordan, Egypt and other Arab states that denied the Palestinians a voice in the armistice negotiations of 1948-49. Nor is it mentioned that the failure to establish the Palestinian state called for in the U.N. Partition Resolution of 1947 was solely a result of political decisions by the Arab states, and not because of any failure of the Israelis to recognize the national rights of the Palestinians.

Neither do the Quaker authors recall that the Palestinian residents of the West Bank expressed militant, often violent, opposition to Trans-Jordan's unilateral action in annexing the West Bank and the Old City of Jerusalem in 1949, and that only two governments—the United Kingdom and Pakistan—ever recognized the Jordanian annexation.

Further, the Quaker document chooses to ignore the record of discrimination against the Palestinians by the government of Jordan during the entire period of Jordanian occupation from 1949 until June 1967. There is no indication of the fact that King Hussein recruited and staffed his army almost entirely from the ranks of the East Bank Bedouins as a means of consolidating his power over the more advanced and separatist-minded West Bank Palestinians. The report does not reveal that special privileges —social, economic and political—were granted the Bedouins, while the seven-year Jordanian Development Plan, 1964-70, was concerned almost exclusively with the advancement of the East Bank, leaving the West Bank Palestinians to little more than subsistence farming.

There is no mention of the facts, evident in Arab public records, that:

—After the murder of King Abdullah in 1951, the Arab Legion (made up primarily of Bedouins) ran amok in East Jerusalem. Official government announcements reported many hangings and spoke of the arrest of 6,300 Palestinians in 1951 and 1952.

—Nine political parties were banned in 1957.

—Fifty anti-government demonstrators were killed by Hussein's security forces and hundreds more wounded in April 1963—including 11 killed and 150 wounded in East Jerusalem alone. During the same period, 26 members of the Jordanian parliament were imprisoned.

—In November 1966, hundreds of persons were wounded and many more arrested after violent demonstrations in West Bank cities.

—Some 300,000 Arabs left the West Bank and East Jerusalem between 1949 and May 1967 as a direct result of persistent unrest and lack of economic opportunity in the area.

The Quaker authors' double-standard of morality—one for Israel, the other for the Arabs—is neatly demonstrated in their legitimization of the fact that Jordan seized and held the West Bank and the Old City of Jerusalem as a direct result of its military invasion of Palestine in 1948. This acquisition of territory by war is calmly accepted with the statement: "To be sure, as the principal nation-state heir of Palestine territory and as host government both east and west of the Jordan River to the largest single block of

Palestinians, the Hashemite Kingdom of Jordan has often been assumed to speak for the Palestinian Arabs." (pp. 68-69)

How Jordan became "the principal nation-state heir of Palestine territory" and what qualities it offers as "host government" to the Palestinians are questions the Palestinians themselves have been asking since 1948. In view of the Palestinians' awareness of the underlying conflict of interest between their own "just recognition" and the economic and territorial aspirations of Jordan and other Arab states, it is surprising that these issues are obscured rather than clarified in the report's approach to this crucial subject.

However, in distinct contrast to the authors' limited treatment of Arab responsibility for the long abuse of the Palestinians, there are repeated statements, innuendos and inferences to the effect that the sorry state of the Palestinians is a result of Israeli policy. The report charges, for example, that "many Israelis and their supporters regard the Palestinians as 'invisible men,' without historical or current claim to national rights." (p. 8) (For a balanced treatment of these issues, see "Self-Determination and the Palestinian Arabs" by Julius Stone, Truman Research Institute, Jerusalem, 1970.)

The historical record shows that when Israel unequivocally accepted the U.N. Partition Resolution of 1947, it not only gave formal recognition to the rights of the Palestinians to an independent state of their own but also committed Israel to cooperative commercial and trade relations with that independent Palestinian state. On October 2, 1947—six months before the State of Israel was established—the Assembly of Palestine Jewry issued this appeal: "The Jewish people extends the hand of sincere friendship and brotherhood to the Arab people and calls them to cooperate as free and equal allies for the sake of peace and progress, for the benefit of their respective countries."

It should be noted that the entire West Bank was occupied and controlled by the government of Jordan from 1948 until June 1967; Gaza was similarly controlled by Egypt. The territory that the Quakers now propose for an independent Palestinian state was, for 19 years, entirely in the hands of Arab governments. Why did it not occur to the Quaker group that the abuse of the Palestinians, especially their statelessness during that 19-year period, might be properly charged to the policies of Arab governments?

Again, the Quaker report after describing the exile of Palestinians following the war of 1948-49 states: "This situation continues . . . despite the U.N. Resolution of December 11, 1948, which establishes their right to choose through the Conciliation Commission whether to return to Israel and live at peace with their neighbors or to resettle elsewhere and accept compensation for lost property and rights." (p. 68) The Quaker statement invokes the U.N. resolution with the clear implication that Israel has refused to comply. This is understandably disconcerting to those who know the history of this resolution.

In fact, the Resolution adopted on December 11, 1948, consists of fourteen interlocking and interdependent paragraphs that spelled out the single, central objective of a peaceful, total Arab-Israel settlement. The operative decision in the resolution was to set up a Conciliation Commission and instruct it to "assist the Governments and authorities to achieve a final settlement of all outstanding questions between them." As the record clearly shows, that Conciliation Commission would not allow the refugee issue to be isolated from all the other issues relevant to a total settlement:

> "The Conciliation Commission, while fully recognizing the importance and extreme urgency of the refugee question, both from the humanitarian and political points of view, did not consider it possible to separate any one problem from the rest of the peace negotiations or from the final peace settlement." (*General Progress Report of the UN Conciliation Commission for Palestine.* 1951, UN Doc. A/1367/ Rev. 1, Chap. 1, Para. 5.)

Indeed, the U.N. Conciliation Commission recognized that unremitting Arab belligerency made the solution of the refugee problem impossible. Meeting in Paris with Arab and Israel delegations in 1951, it submitted a comprehensive pattern of proposals for a settlement, with this explanation:

> ". . . (it) had considered that any solution of the refugee question would involve important commitments by Israel. But it had also considered that Israel could not be expected to make such commitments, unless at the same time, she received reasonable assurance from her neighbors as to her national and economic security." (*Progress Report of the UN Conciliation Commission for Palestine, UN Doc. A/1985, para. 21.)*

In an earlier paragraph (Para. 3) of the same document, the

Conciliation Commission publicly and strongly urged that Egypt, Jordan, Syria and Lebanon first join with Israel in signing a "Declaration of Pacific Intentions" committing them to "respect each other's rights to security and freedom from attack, to refrain from warlike or hostile acts against one another, and to promote the return of permanent peace in Palestine."

The Arab states refused to sign the "Declaration of Pacific Intentions."

Nowhere in the Quaker authors' history of the conflict or of the refugee problem are these findings of the Conciliation Commission mentioned. Nowhere is there any acknowledgment that the continuation of the refugee problem might have been due at least as much to the intransigence of the Arab states on the issue of real peace with Israel as to any policy of the Israeli government.

### *The Al Fatah Dream*

Perhaps the single most puzzling aspect of the Quaker report's description of the Palestinian Arab position relates to their treatment of what is described as "The Al Fatah Dream."

> "There is no agreement among Palestinians, either refugees or those living under Israeli occupation, upon a single preferred course of action. To Al Fatah, largest of the resistance organizations, and to some of the rival groups, the possibility of peace is linked directly with the dissolution of the present state of Israel. They call for the creation of a secular, multi-religious state in which Arabs and Jews can live as fellow-citizens within a democratic system. . . . They specifically deny any intention, formerly expressed by Arab extremists, to 'throw the Jews into the sea.' " (p. 69)

This description of the Al Fatah position is presented at face value by the Quaker authors. Moreover, it is put forward as representing the most extreme Palestinian point of view.

On the basis of the historical record, the report's description of the Palestinian Arab positions is both disarmingly moderate and unaccountably incomplete. The consistent Palestinian demand for total and exclusive possession of the entire territory, including all of Israel, is simply omitted. This demand for total and exclusive possession was evidenced in the Palestinians' opposition to the 1947 U.N. Partition Plan. It appears today in the demand for "total liberation" and sovereignty over the whole territory of Palestine. While there may be "divergent and moderate views," the primary expression of Palestinian aspirations has focussed on their refusal (and that of the Arab states) to recognize the right of the Jews to a separate national existence—even in a small portion of the original Palestine Mandate territory.

This absolute position is set forth with complete clarity by the Palestinian "resistance" groups. They vehemently oppose any political settlement, regardless of boundaries or conditions, because their opposition is to the principle of a Jewish state of any size or shape.

The Palestinians formulated this opposition in their National Covenant, first adopted in 1964, and then amended by their Congress in Cairo of July, 1968. Representatives of all the Palestinian organizations participated in the Congress. The National Covenant was approved by Al Fatah and most of the other terrorist groups and reinforced with explicit resolutions. Concurrence with it is a condition for joining the "Command of Armed Struggle." The National Covenant is the Palestinians' basic political document. But you will find no reference to it or mention of it in the Quakers' *Search for Peace in the Middle East.*

Article 21 of the Covenant asserts: "The Palestinian Arab people, in expressing itself through the armed Palestinian revolution, rejects every solution that is a substitute for the complete liberation of Palestine. . . ." The right of self-determination is defined, by the Convenant, as the right of "restoring" the whole territory of Palestine. This means that the Jews now living in the country have no right of national self-determination.

It is important to note that in the first version of the Covenant, adopted in May of 1964, the Jews who lived in Palestine in 1947 would have been recognized as Palestinians and would have been allowed to remain. In the July 1968 revision by the fourth session of the National Council, still in force, it is explicitly stated that only Jews who lived permanently in Palestine before 1917 would be recognized as Palestinians. This means that almost two and a half million Jews would be banished from the land.

Although, according to the Quaker report, Al Fatah and other groups "specifically deny any intention, formerly expressed by Arab extremists, to 'throw the Jews into the sea,'" the Palestinian Covenant would appear to encompass an equally radical solution to the problem of Israel and its citizens. Only now it is left to the imagination; each reader of the Covenant can speculate for himself how the new Palestinian State will rid itself of the two and one-half million Jews who have no right to be there.

Apparently, however, hearing Arabs mouth such words as "secular," "multi-religious" and "democratic," and hearing them utter such phrases as "We are prepared to live at peace in a re-united Palestine with our Jewish neighbors" (p. 70) so bemused the Quaker authors that they blithely accepted these Arab assurances of good intentions toward the Jews, even though the Al Fatah calls for a "Holy War" to achieve its ends. But they have considerable explaining to do for equally blithely ignoring the very existence of the landmark document known as the Palestinian Covenant.

(In order that our readers may obtain a clear understanding of the contents and spirit of the National Covenant, we include its complete text with an analysis in Appendix II.)

## CHAPTER VIII

# THE GOVERNMENT OF ISRAEL AND ISRAELI POLICY

In many places and in many ways, the Quaker report is sharply critical of the government of Israel and the policies the Quakers ascribe to it. Some of the criticisms are examined below.

> "Both Israeli and Arab governments have been long wedded to a no-compromise line and to strident propaganda attacks on the other side." (p. 46)

This seemingly even-handed indictment, which appears in several parts of the Quaker report, requires some elaboration. In fact, the substance of the Israeli and Arab "no-compromise" lines are quite different. Yet the Quaker report equates Israel's insistence on a meaningful final peace agreement signed by the Arab states with the persistent refusal of the Arab states to accept the idea of a binding and final treaty of peace. Similarly, the Quaker report equates Israel's initial insistence on direct negotiations—which have always characterized post-war peace negotiations among nation states—with the Arab refusal to engage in such efforts. According to the report, both positions represent a "no compromise" line which is to be condemned. This simple-minded even-handedness is the best treatment Israel receives from the Quaker report. Much of the rest of it simply accepts Arab intransigence as a "given" to which Israel must accommodate itself, as if the fact of losing the Six-Day War had granted the Arab states a kind of moral superiority. For example, the report blandly accepts the position that the Arab states are somehow exempt from the procedures which, by international experience and practice, have elsewhere been considered as normal. This is what the Quakers say:

> "It is the judgment of the authors of this paper that direct bilateral negotiations are not possible as the way to settle the Arab-Israeli conflict. Neither side feels strong enough to have genuinely free and comprehensive negotiations." (p. 87)

In view of the fact that Israel has consistently urged direct bilateral negotiations as the only way to settle the Middle East conflict (for which it has been sharply criticized by the authors of the Quaker report, among others) this "judgment of the authors" is puzzling. Indeed, as the public record so clearly shows, all of the reluctance to engage in direct negotiations has been on the Arab side. It is both erroneous and misleading to attribute a fear of direct negotiations to both sides. Indeed, on this point the Quaker report serves merely to excuse the Arabs' pointed refusal to meet the Israelis in direct negotiations. Only if Israel does not merit the same sovereign right accorded to any other nation-state that has fought a war and now seeks to establish a peace can the Arabs' rejection of direct negotiations be justified.

Whatever else can be said about the report's definition of the "no-compromise line," the charge that each side is equally guilty of "strident propaganda attacks on the other side" is simply not supported by the historical record.

Over the years, the custom among apologists for the Arab cause has been to counter the embarrassing Arab use of blood-chilling imagery by explaining it as "merely rhetorical extravagance used for home consumption in the somewhat primitive Arab states." The record of such "strident propaganda attacks" by the Arabs on Israel is voluminous. "To drive the Jews into the sea" is but one of many variations on the oft-recorded theme of annhilation of the Jews. Others involve: "Jihad," the Holy War against the infidels; "purification" of the Holy Land; the "liquidation" of Israel; "de-Zionization" of Palestine, etc., etc.

These violent expressions from official leaders of Arab governments and their mass media have been accompanied by a host of charges and allegations designed to whip up and maintain a fervor of anti-Israel vituperation. Some typical examples:

*President Nasser of Egypt:*

"We will act to realize Arab solidarity and the closing of the ranks that will eventually put an end to Israel. . . . We will liquidate her." (August 17, 1961)

"The Arab national aim is the elimination of Israel." (May 25, 1965)

"We will not accept any . . . co-existence with Israel . . . Today the issue is not the establishment of peace between the Arab states and Israel . . . The war with Israel is in effect since 1948." (May 28, 1967)

*Falastin,* a Jordanian daily:

"It would appear, on the face of it, that the concentration of the Jews in the Occupied Region militates in favor of Zionism. In our view, it will favor the Arab nation . . . because this will turn Israel into one huge, worldwide grave for this whole Jewish concentration. And the day draws near for those who await it." (March 3, 1963)

*Syrian Officials:*

"The Syrian army stands as a mountain to crush Israel and demolish her. This army knows how to crush its enemies."—Defense Minister Abdullah Ziada. (August 19, 1963)

"Our army will be satisfied with nothing less than the disappearance of Israel."—Commander-in-Chief Salah Jadid. (October 30, 1964)

"We want total war with no limits, a war that will destroy the Zionist base."—President Nurredin Al-Attassi. (May 22, 1966)

*King Hussein of Jordan:*

"Jordan, with its Left and Right Bank, is the ideal jumping ground to liberate the usurped homeland." (April 12, 1964)

*Ahmed Shukairy, Chairman of the Palestine Liberation Organization:*

"D-Day is approaching. The Arabs have waited 19 years for this and will not flinch from the war of liberation." (May 26, 1967)

"This is a fight for the homeland—it is either us or the Israelis. There is no middle road. The Jews of Palestine will have to leave. We will facilitate their departure to their former homes. Any of the old Palestinian Jewish population who survive may stay, but it is my impression that none of them will survive." (June 1, 1967)

The above quotations, all made before the Six-Day War, show that Arab leaders spoke with little inhibition of their aim to liquidate the State of Israel. But the genocidal threats which poured so freely from the Arab capitals evoked criticism from many parts of the world. To counter this criticism, since 1967 Arab propaganda has been somewhat toned down and often replaced by more sophisticated locutions. Threats of genocide were largely put aside and replaced with the theme of politicide. For example, the Arabs would not liquidate the Jews; they would merely "de-

Zionize" Palestine. Once the real meaning of "de-Zionization" is clarified, however, the operational distinction from the earlier Arab propaganda theme of genocide becomes non-existent.

> "Israel makes no sense, geographically or economically . . . The battle which began on 5 June will then become only one battle in what will be a long war."—King Hussein of Jordan (June 26, 1967)

> "On behalf of all the Arab delegations, and in accordance with the resolution adopted by the League of Arab States, we now confirm, as we have stated in the past, our non-recognition of the State of Israel . . . The denial of recognition to that State should be reaffrmed time and again."—George Tomeh, Syrian Representative to U.N. (July 17, 1967)

> "The Arab heads of state have agreed to unite their political efforts at the international and diplomatic level . . . This will be done within the framework of the main principles by which the Arab States abide, namely: No peace with Israel, no recognition of Israel, no negotiations with Israel . . ."—Resolutions of Khartoum Arab Summit Conference (Aug. 24-Sept. 1, 1967)

> "The Arabs will adhere to the Khartoum Summit Conference decision of no peace, no recognition and no negotiations with Israel." —President Nasser (Nov. 23, 1967)

> "The Arab struggle aims at liquidating the results of the June '67 aggression without losing sight of the aim of liquidating the results of the aggression of May '48."—*Al-Ahram,* Cairo daily (Dec. 29, 1967)

> "The real Palestine problem is the existence of Israel in Palestine. As long as a Zionist existence remains even in a tiny part of it— that will mean occupation. The important thing is to liquidate the Israel occupation, and there is no difference between the territories lately occupied and those occupied before."—Voice of the Arabs, Radio Cairo (March 17, 1968)

> "Israel . . . should definitely be annihilated."—President el-Bakr of Iraq (April 2, 1968)

> "The Arab nation has decided to embark on the path of struggle and war . . . We will move on to the containment of Israel, and after that to . . . its eradication."—President Nasser (April 10, 1968)

> "We are in favor of the liquidation of the Zionist regime."—Representative of Algeria in U.N. Security Council (May 1, 1968)

> ". . . Her [Israel's] one hope is to obtain acceptance by the Arabs

of her existence and their consent to cooperate with her. It is here that the significance and importance of the Arab rejection appears." —Hassanein Haikal, editor of *Al-Ahram* (June 1, 1968)

"The first and paramount aim of the Arab nation, including the Egyptian people, is the unification of all its forces and resources in order to cleanse the Arab land and liberate it. This is an unquestioned aim, and there is no alternative to it, whatever the difficulties and sacrifices."—President Nasser (July 5, 1968)

"There can be no political solution short of complete Israeli evacuation of Palestine . . ."—President Nurredin Al-Attassi (Nov. 11, 1968)

"The military preparations [for restoring our losses] need not disrupt our political preparations. But it will be dangerous if we let the political preparations disrupt the military ones. For in the end one truth will remain in the Middle East arena, one exclusive truth, that will not be doubted, one clean and spotless truth, that is: the necessity to restore our land and purify it to the last inch—a full and final purification."—President Nasser (Feb. 1, 1969)

In the face of this brief sampling of Arab invective, there is not one single statement or implication by spokesmen for the Israeli government that threatens the destruction of any Arab state.

The Quaker report does not quote any of the innumerable Arab propaganda attacks but does cite a statement by the then Israeli Prime Minister, Levi Eshkol, warning the Syrians in April 1967, that they would face "measures no less drastic than those of April 7" should they continue their unprovoked attacks across the Israeli border. The measures of April 7 involved a Syrian-initiated border incident which ultimately led to the shooting down of six Syrian planes over Damascus.

Is this what the Quaker report means by "strident propaganda attacks" on the part of Israel? But even the Quaker authors must recognize that the promise of reprisals for any projected attack by the enemy is quite different from threatening to annihilate the nation-state of that enemy. Neither in the war of 1948, nor in 1956, nor in 1967 was it ever Israel's policy or intention to eliminate the national life of any Arab state. Indeed, the limitless record of provocative propaganda attacks made against Israel by leaders and governments of the Arab world during the past 22 years is matched only by the number of conciliatory and peace-seeking statements made by the Israeli government and leaders during the same period. In addition to the statement issued by the Assembly of Palestine Jewry six months before the founding of Israel extending "friendship and brotherhood to the Arab peoples" and calling on them "to cooperate as free and equal allies for the sake of peace and progress," Israel's Proclamation of Independence, issued May 14, 1948, declared:

> "In the midst of wanton aggression, we yet call upon the Arab inhabitants of the State of Israel to return to the ways of peace and to play their part in the development of the State, with full and equal citizenship and due representation in all its bodies and institutions, provisional or permanent."

From an address by Golda Meir, then Israel's Foreign Minister, before the U.N. General Assembly on October 9, 1962:

> "My government rejects war as a means of settling disputes. From the day that the State of Israel was established, my government has called for settling all outstanding differences by direct negotiations.
>
> "The policy of the Israeli Government has been and continues to be peace. It is peace, not only for the world, but also between us and our neighbors. We believe in co-existence and cooperation everywhere and we shall do everything in our power towards that end . . .
>
> "Despite all the speeches which we have heard from Arab representatives, we are convinced that for us and for our neighbors the day must come when we shall live in amity and cooperation. Then will the entire Middle East become a region where the tens of millions of people will dwell in peace and then will its economic potentialities and rich cultural heritage achieve fulfillment."

Foreign Minister Abba Eban at U.N. General Assembly, June 19, 1967:

> "Free from external pressures and interventions, imbued with a common love for a region which they are destined to share, the Arab and Jewish nations must now transcend their conflicts in dedication to a new Mediterranean future . . .
>
> "The development of arid zones, the desalination of water and the conquest of tropical disease are common interests of the entire region, congenial to a sharing of knowledge and experience.

". . . young Israelis and Arabs could join in a mutual discourse of learning. The old prejudices could be replaced by a new comprehension and respect . . . In such a Middle East, military budgets would spontaneously find a less exacting point of equilibrium. Excessive sums devoted to security could be diverted to development projects.

"For the first time in history, no Mediterranean nation is in subjection. All are endowed with sovereign freedom. The challenge now is to use this freedom for creative growth. There is only one road to that end. It is the road of recognition, of direct contact, of true cooperation. It is the road of peaceful co-existence.

"In free negotiation with each of our neighbors, we shall offer durable and just solutions redounding to our mutual advantage and honor."

Prime Minister Levi Eshkol at Sharm el Sheikh, June 20, 1967:

"I am ready to meet our nearest neighbors, President Nasser, King Hussein and other Arab leaders, at any place and at any time in order to hold peace talks.

"We want to forget what was done to us. We want to prevent future tests of strength, and we want Jews and Arabs to renew those bright days when together we contributed to human culture. There is a great future in store for the Middle East. We must not miss this opportunity . . ."

Yigal Allon, Cabinet Minister, February 18, 1968:

"The Arabs should test Israel at the bargaining table, as they did on the battlefield . . . There are no problems that cannot be solved by talks. Israel is ready to sit with them."

The above quotations are only a small sample, but they are representative.

The facts in the public record then, are that (a) while there are innumerable examples of provocative and "strident" propaganda attacks made by official Arab spokesmen against Israel, there are no remotely comparable attacks made by official Israeli spokesmen against the Arabs; (b) while there are innumerable examples of conciliatory and peace-seeking statements made by official Israeli spokesmen towards the Arabs, there are no remotely comparable conciliatory statements toward Israel made by official spokesmen of the Arab belligerents.

It is mystifying that the Quaker report could overlook the overwhelming weight of evidence from the public record that dramatizes the sharp and undeniable differences between Arab and Israeli "propaganda." Significantly, what the authors term "strident propaganda" was often not "propaganda" at all but a clear and sober statement of basic Arab intentions. That many of the threats of genocide against the Jews of Israel by Arab leaders were not merely "propaganda" is convincingly evidenced by the Arabs' repeated attempts to implement that policy from 1948 to 1967. Indeed, only Israel's determination and ability to resist the Arab onslaughts prevented that "propaganda" from becoming historical fact. When the President of Syria says "Israel . . . should definitely be annihilated," it cannot be taken merely as "strident propaganda"—given Syria's determined efforts to do just that from 1948 until today.

The Quaker authors' failure to recognize the glaring difference in tone, attitude and aspiration between Arab and Israeli public statements and postures leads one to question how much faith is to be placed in their ability to judge objectively between the Arabs and Israel on more complex and subtle issues. Thus, the report declares:

> ". . . through the 1940's and well into the 1950's, there . . . remained only an uneasy truce, broken occasionally by acts of terror and counter-terror." (p. 27)
>
> "Most of these refugee-commando attacks were mounted from Jordan or Syria. . . . The Syrians . . . openly supported the Palestinian commandos, while Syrian army artillery lobbed shells, month after month, from the ridges of the Golan Heights into nearby Israeli agricultural settlements. Efforts inside the United Nations to halt these attacks, or even to censure the Arab governments for allowing them, were regularly vetoed by the Soviet Union. On the other hand, when Israel struck back—as she did from time to time, and often on a massive 'two-eyes-for-an-eye' basis, the United Nations promptly condemned her." (p. 31)
>
> "Arab terrorism creates immediate Israeli reaction—often on the basis of 'two eyes for an eye.' " (p. 82)

The Quaker report almost invariably couples Arab "terror" with "counter-terror" by the Israelis. "Terror" and "counter-terror" are accorded precisely the same treatment. To ignore the substantial difference between acts of terror initiated by one side and counter-actions designed to halt or discourage such terror by the other side is to judge the policeman as guilty as the criminal. The Quaker report never distinguishes the essential difference between the two.

By any definition, the acts of Arab terrorists—mining farm roads and fields, placing bombs in supermarkets, movie houses, university libraries and bus stations, sending bazooka shells into a school bus at close range, firing katyusha rockets into cities, towns and villages—are properly labeled "terror." But the very nature of Israeli counter-actions make the use of a word like "counter-terror" inaccurate and inappropriate. While one of the admitted purposes of the counter-actions was to discourage and inhibit further terrorist attacks on civilian targets, the Israeli responses were with no significant exception planned and carried out against legitimate military targets—terrorist bases or military installations where the Syrian or Jordanian military had been involved in the provocation.

In Syria, Egypt and Jordan, both regular military and terrorist groups had established operational bases in the midst of civilian enclaves. Thus, an Israeli attack on legitimate military targets could involve hazards to civilian life and property. (This was demonstrated by the campaign of the Jordanian Army against the Palestinian rebels in September 1970. Artillery fire was directed point-blank into refugee camps, where Palestinians had deliberately located their positions.) The record is clear that Israel's counter-actions were planned and executed to achieve certain distinct and limited goals, with minimal hazard to innocent civilian life. Their nature was entirely different from the Arab terror; to describe them as "counter-terror" is to twist the meaning of words. Yet these fairly obvious distinctions, although fully documented in the historical record, go unnoticed in the Quaker report. "Terror" and "counter-terror" are used as if they were descriptions of the same abhorrent destructive will, equally characteristic of both Arab terrorists and the Israeli defense forces.

It is interesting to note that only Israel's counter-actions lead the Quakers repeatedly to use perjorative rhetoric: "often on a massive 'two-eyes-for-an-eye' basis"; "often on the basis of 'two eyes for an eye' "; etc. In contrast, the terrorist attacks are described as "refugee-commando" attacks (see above), clearly suggesting a not inconsiderable measure of sympathy and understanding for their alleged origin. There is no word in the entire report about terrorist excesses even though their attacks are virtually always directed against civilian—not military—targets.

Considering the cumulative record of death and destruction wreaked by Arab terror against Israeli civilian targets prior to any single Israeli reprisal raid, it seems strange to label the Israeli counter-actions as based on "two eyes for an eye."

Another illustration of the Quaker group's views concerning Israeli policy is the following quotation:

> "It is also our judgment that the Israeli government should abandon its policy of massive retaliatory 'over-kill' strikes against Arab targets and give up its preventive attacks on far-ranging military targets in the United Arab Republic, in Jordan, and in Syria. It is essential that a cease-fire be maintained . . ." (p. 82)

Here the Quakers again attribute to the government of Israel a deliberate policy of "over-kill"—like the "two eyes for an eye" allegation in their discussion of Israel's counter-actions to Arab terror. But putting aside the issue of why the report's pejoratives are reserved exclusively for Israel, a serious question arises from the way in which basic facts and the sequence of events from 1967-1970 are ignored or glossed-over.

There is a clear and available public record which spells out the three-stage Egyptian program promulgated by President Nasser for dealing with Israel after the Arabs' defeat in June 1967: *Stage 1,* the rebuilding and re-equipment of Egypt's military power in the period immediately following the 1967 June debacle; *Stage 2,* a "war of attrition" against Israel's forces on the Suez Ceasefire Line; *Stage 3,* the invasion of the Sinai and "liberation" of the entire territory, including all of Israel.

> "We will step up our military activity under conditions and in circumstances convenient to us. . . . The political fight is merely a rung on the ladder of force. When the time comes, we will strike." (President Nasser, Radio Cairo, November 23, 1967)

> "The Arab nation has decided to embark on the path of struggle and war. . . . We will move on to the containment of Israel, and after that to . . . its eradication." (President Nasser, Radio Cairo, April 10, 1968)

> "The fierce artillery battle is an important point in the military confrontation with Israel." (*Al-Ahram,* government-controlled Cairo daily, September 9, 1968)

> "The time has passed when we required that any soldier at the front who opened fire on the enemy should have to account for that, because we wanted to avoid complications. Now the picture is different . . . Now, if a soldier at the front sees the enemy and does not open fire, we call him to account for that." (President Nasser, Radio Cairo, March 10, 1969)

> "Egypt no longer considers itself bound by the 1967 cease-fire agreement with Israel." (Egyptian Government Spokesman Muhammad Hassan al-Zayat, Cairo, April 23, 1969)

The U.S.S.R.'s massive airlift to Egypt of weapons and technicians in the months immediately following the Arabs' June 1967 debacle, and the systematic rearming and retraining program that followed, brought Egypt's armed forces within a period of 18 months to a strength surpassing their 1967 peak. In the early spring of 1969, Nasser declared a unilateral abrogation of the U.N. cease-fire with the announced goal "to exhaust and bleed Israel." Nasser's war of attrition was made possible only by the Soviet Union's guarantee of the guns, ammunition and other resources required for its prosecution. The Egyptian assumption, clearly stated by Nasser, was that heavy bombardment across the Suez line would cause such casualties and require such an expenditure of scant Israeli resources that Israel would be forced to retreat—preparing the ground for the next phase—the crossing of the Suez in force and the "eradication" of Israel.

Vastly outnumbered in manpower and artillery, and facing a growing casualty toll after three months of heavy Egyptian bombardment, Israel undertook a program of measured air strikes against Egyptian military targets in an effort to reduce its losses, scale down the fighting and force the restoration of the Suez cease-fire.

This record is available to any observer. But the Quaker authors do not mention Egypt's unilateral abrogation of the Suez cease-fire and they refrain from any condemnation of an act which not only violated the U.N. cease-fire agreement (which the government of Egypt had formally approved and accepted) but also catapulted the entire region into a renewed frenzy of military escalation and produced a threat against the peace unequalled by the action of any other nation. Yet on this vital component of the whole issue of war and peace, the Quaker report is mute.

Just as the report neglects to mention Egypt's action in abrogating its solemn obligation to maintain the cease-fire, so does it omit any condemnation of the actions of the governments of Jordan and Syria in permitting and indeed encouraging the wanton bombardment aimed at Israeli civilian targets by both terrorists and regular military forces.

On the other hand, directly or by implication and innuendo, the Quaker group has no hesitation in criticizing the policies of Israel and Israel's Jewish supporters in the U.S.:

> ". . . the more prominent American Jewish organizational leadership, the people whom Israeli and American Jewish dissidents call the American Jewish establishment, tend to give vigorous personal and organizational support to hard-line policies within the Israeli government and to urge the United States public and the American government to do the same." (p. 89)

> "The Israeli government and people continue to brush aside the commando attacks as having no more military significance than traffic accidents, regrettable though bearable, but they serve to unify a loose coalition government that would otherwise fly apart and bind an otherwise critical and peace-hungry people to the hard-line policies of the government." (p. 96)

> ". . . there is a tendency for some of the leaders of the American Jewish establishment to identify themselves with the more hard-line elements inside the Israeli cabinet, and to ignore or discount the dissident elements, in and out of the Israeli government, that are searching for more creative ways to solve the Middle East problems." (p. 117)

These statements and others scattered throughout the report clearly reveal the Quaker group's basic attitude and conclusions on several very important points. These can be summarized as follows:

(1) The government of Israel is committed to "hard-line" policies. (2) Except for the "commando" attacks on Israel, the "loose coalition" government would fly apart because the people of Israel are "peace-hungry," divided about their government and critical of its policies. (3) There is also an unfortunate tendency for the "American Jewish establishment" to support the hard-line government, when really it should be identifying with the "dissident ele-

ments" that are "searching for more creative ways to solve the Middle East problems."

The Quaker authors never really define what they describe as the "hard-line" policies of the Israeli government. That accusatory description is simply used without clarification. From the context of the report as a whole, however, we may conclude that the authors' criticism relates mainly to (1) Israel's insistence on direct negotiations as the best way to achieve agreement among the states concerned on the issues that divide them; (2) Israel's insistence that the November 22, 1967 U.N. Resolution does not require withdrawal from all the occupied territories; and (3) Israel's insistence that equal emphasis be given to Paragraph 2, Article 1 of the U.N. resolution which specifies the right of every state in the area "to live in peace within secure and recognized boundaries."

If the Quaker authors see these Israeli positions as being "hard-line," how then do they describe the official Arab line adopted at the Arab summit conference in Khartoum on September 1, 1967, which states: "No peace with Israel, no recognition of Israel, no negotiations with Israel." This major Arab Resolution—certainly a significant and key pronouncement—is simply omitted by the authors of the report.

Whether or not one accepts the judgment that Israel is committed to an unduly "hard-line" policy, the report's allegation that the government does not have the support of the Israeli people goes counter to all the evidence.

The Israeli political system is a parliamentary democracy whose very existence depends on the support of the citizenry. As in Britain, when the government does not have the confidence of the people, new elections are held to offer the people a choice of new leadership. "Dissident elements" are free to oppose and criticize the policies of the governing majority in Israel as in other free and democratic countries. The Quakers were perhaps too readily impressed by "dissident" voices in Israel. The views they quote and endorse are in fact held only by a tiny minority. Like dissident elements in other free countries, they often have the facility for making themselves heard out of all proportion to their numbers or real influence with the people. But the Quaker group hears only what it wants.

Israel's free press, with its more than 23 separate and independent newspapers, makes these facts easily ascertainable. Despite dissent and debate over a host of domestic issues, on the consuming issue of international policy the Israeli people firmly support their government, and are convinced that their government is every bit as "peace-hungry" as they are for real and lasting peace. Indeed, every public opinion poll conducted in Israel in the past three years confirms that conclusion. And the popularity polls, taken from time to time by many newspapers and other opinion research groups, show consistently that Prime Minister Golda Meir is by far the most popular personality in Israel. One measure of public support for the government's policy may be seen in the fact that the number of requests for conscientious-objector status, despite the available opportunities for noncombatant alternatives, is extremely small.

If opposition and dissenting views are to be considered as representative of significant popular departures from government policy, the fact is that opposition from the "right"—the less flexible and more "hard-line" Israeli parties—has far more public support than opposition from the "left." The Gahal Party, which quit the government coalition in early summer 1970 rather than accept the U.S. initiative for a renewed Suez cease-fire, is far more significant by any measure of public influence than any of the splinter groups whose views are apparently more agreeable to the Quaker authors. In the Knesset (the Israeli parliament) the parties supporting the government position hold 77 out of the 120 seats. The parties advocating a "harder" line on the Arab question hold 38 seats. The parties whose views come closest to those of the authors of the Quaker report (the Communists and New Left parties) hold only 5 seats. This breakdown of public opinion is corroborated by an Israeli Institute of Public Opinion poll which measured public reaction to the views expressed by Prime Minister Golda Meir in an interview with the London *Times* on March 13, 1971. The poll showed that 57 percent of the respondents fully supported Mrs. Meir, 38 percent criticized her for her willingness to make so many concessions, and only 5 percent felt she was being too extreme in her demands.

The report's characterization of the Israeli government as a "loose coalition" is tendentious, as is the assertion (for which no evidence is offered) that only the "commando" attacks prevent the Israeli government from flying apart. "Coalition government" means only that no single political party controls a parliamentary (Knesset) majority. One can hardly impugn the representative nature or stability of the Israeli government by noting the acknowledged fact that there are differences of opinion in the Israeli Cabinet. There are similar differences, after all, to be found in every free government (including the U.S.) and every free institution (including, hopefully, the American Friends Service Committee).

Finally, the Quaker authors obviously misinterpret the relationships of the "American Jewish establishment" to the government and politics of Israel. The Israelis are indeed "a highly individualistic people"—but they are equally a very independent people. They undoubtedly value the support and commitment of American Jews to the cause of Israel's survival and progress, but they will not tolerate any semblance of interference in their politics and state policies by the "American Jewish establishment" or by any other foreigners. When the Quaker report glibly asserts that "the more prominent American Jewish organizational leadership, the people whom Israeli and American Jewish dissidents call the American Jewish establishment, tend to give vigorous personal and organizational support to hard-line policies within the Israel government," it demonstrates a regrettable lack of knowledge about both American Jewish organizations and the workings of the Israeli government—and an apparent reliance on the unsubstantiated allegations of some "Israeli and American Jewish dissidents."

The inescapable conclusion to be drawn from the statements in the report on Israel's "hard-line" attitude is that they underline the authors' basic hostility to the government of Israel. Their advice to the "American Jewish establishment" reflects not only the naive presumption that with American Jewish support the "dissidents" would become a dominant voice in the determination of Israeli policy but also (as we shall see below) an implicit threat to the American Jewish community.

At the very least, the Quaker authors' attitude is unseemly if not counter-productive to any search for peace in the Middle East, since the government of Israel presumably will have to be a party to that peace. Even more glaring, however, is the fact that with all the unflattering attention given to the government of Israel, there is not a comparable word of criticism in the entire Quaker report of the government of any Arab state or of the Soviet Union.

The fact is that most of the Arab governments are military dictatorships, permitting few if any democratic freedoms. This apparently does not offend the Quaker authors' political or moral sensibilities, for they make no comment on it nor do they mention it, The "American Jewish establishment" is fair game for the Quaker authors because of its support of Israel's "hard-line" policies. The Arab "establishment"—where an oligarchy has preeminent privilege and unlimited control of political, social and economic power—has not yet been discovered by the same authors, who seem to be blind in one eye.

## CHAPTER IX

# SUGGESTIONS FOR A PRACTICAL PEACE SETTLEMENT

Having endorsed the Arab propaganda line that Israel was created by the West and imposed on the Arabs, "who were being required to pay for the anti-Semitic sins of the Christian West" (p. 24), the report asserts that "anti-Jewish prejudices, discrimination and persecution are not a problem which the Arab countries must be expected to solve for the rest of the world by repeatedly trading away Arab territory." (p. 94) The strategy of distortion now becomes clear. By neglecting the true history of Israel's rise and by avoiding the root causes of the three wars that Israel fought for its survival (1948, 1956 and 1967), the authors are able to portray the Arab countries as innocent victims of Western guilt and the existence of Israel as an injustice against the Arabs.

This is the real meaning of the report's statement that the world problem of anti-Jewish prejudice cannot be resolved "by repeatedly trading away Arab territory." This statement effectively denies all Jewish claims to any part of Palestine because it is "Arab" territory that is being traded away. Thus do the authors give implicit assent to the Arab propaganda line that the very existence of the State of Israel is an act of aggression against the Arab world.

To bring matters up-to-date, the report brackets this basic historical distortion with warnings (undocumented) of Arab "convictions" about "an inevitable continuing Jewish expansionist drive." (p. 94) The authors then express their own understanding of this fixation in terms of "the sometimes explicit, sometimes merely hinted references of Israeli leaders to a continuing in-gathering of Jews from all over the world. . . ." (pp. 94-95)

In the absence of any convincing evidence of Jewish "expansionism," the authors raise the issue indirectly by expressing their concern about "the in-gathering of Jews." It should be noted, however, that while the report seeks to give this principle a semi-secret, almost conspiratorial tone ("sometimes explicit, sometimes merely hinted"), the fact is that the in-gathering of those Jews who choose to come to Israel is one of the cardinal principles on which the Jewish state was founded. Why do the Quaker authors make it sound less than open and honest? And why, in view of the facts, do they choose to interpert the in-gathering as tied to "an expansion of the Jewish-held territories in the Middle East at the expense of the Arabs?"

The answers to these questions are not hard to find. The Quaker report seeks to advance the view that Israel is both aggressive and expansionist, and therefore guilty of creating an Arab "sense of fear, hopelessness, and resentment that overclouds all attempts at rational discussion of a Middle East settlement." (p. 95)

The facts, however, are clear enough. Israel accepted the U.N. Partition Plan of 1947, despite its serious disappointments for the Jews; the Arabs rejected it. Israel fought three wars to defend its very life; all were instigated by the Arab states. Israel opened its gates to Jews the world over; its policy was (and remains) predicated not on the acquisition of more territory but on continued reclamation of wastelands, especially the Negev, and further development of high-technology industries.

Nevertheless, the Quaker authors extend their contrary implications and innuendos:

> "All Israeli leaders insist that it was not any Jewish territorial ambition that produced the June War or that would stand in the way of peace now. However, having acquired new territories as the result of that war, many Israelis do not want to give them back and some indicate they want even more. Only a forthright declaration by the Israeli government repudiating the accusation that its plans for Jewish immigration are tied to any further demands for territorial expansion can begin to allay the most persistent Arab fears." (p. 95)

The negative implications and nuances of this paragraph to the contrary notwithstanding, it should have been clear to the Quaker authors, as it is to most of the rest of the world, that the position of the Israeli government is for withdrawal (that is, return of Arab territories) to "secure and agreed boundaries." The Israeli government has no need of "repudiating the accusation" that it has any "further demands for territorial expansion." (This kind of charge is best described as the "when-did-you-stop-beating-your-wife?" syndrome; it is regrettable that the Quaker authors stooped to it.) There is not a single instance of Israel's ever having made such demands: we may rest assured that had there been any such evidence, the authors of the report would not have hesitated to cite it.

But all of this was not unknown to the Quaker group. In fact, in an exchange with Judge Justine Wise Polier and other representatives of the American Jewish Congress, at a meeting held on February 4, 1971, at his own request, Dr. Landrum Bolling, editor of the Quaker report, "acknowledged that Israel was not interested in territorial expansion and was concerned only in achieving secure borders as essential to peace. He acknowledged that, in contrast, the Arabs continued to be hostile toward the very existence of Israel in the Middle East. When he was pressed to explain why the vast difference in these two positions had not been stated, his only answer was that to have done so would have barred a return to Cairo and the continuation of the dialogue." (*Congress Bi-Weekly,* April 2, 1971, p. 7.)

This further evidence of the Quaker authors' "pro-Arab slant" exposes an unfortunate disregard for truth and fairness. But the report adds insult to injury by equating "Arab paranoia over the prospects of unlimited Israeli territorial expansion" with "a Jewish paranoia towards the prospects of unceasing Arab determination to destroy Israel and to slaughter all Jews." (p. 95)

Since paranoia is a psychosis involving only delusions of persecution and irrational suspicions, this evenhanded diagnosis is ludicrous. The Quaker authors are here equating Israel's actual experience of three wars launched by Arabs whose stated purpose was annihilation of the Jews with the Arabs' alleged "fears" of a Jewish policy for which there is no objective evidence and against which, as the report concedes, "all Israeli leaders" have testified. The report's call for "first steps toward a settlement," which would lead to the establishment of "mutual credibility" between Arabs and Jews, is burdened by the issue of the Quaker authors' own credibility.

But all of this distortion is necessary to "justify" the conclusion that the steps to peace require that:

"First, the Israeli government must give forthright assurances on eventual withdrawal from occupied territories as part of an overall peace settlement and should attempt to refute accusations of further expansionist aims."

The first step to peace, in this view, must be an Israeli commitment to withdraw from occupied territories. As we have seen, the authors' interpretation, like the Russian-Arab interpretation, means withdrawal from all the territories. In fact, a few pages later (p. 99), more precise phraseology is employed: "Israel must make firm commitments for withdrawal from territories occupied after June 5, 1967."

In addition, as part of the first step, Israel must "attempt to refute accusations of further expansionist aims." (Again, what further expansionist aims? And how do the authors suggest this unfounded accusation be refuted?)

In return for Israel's commitment to return to the same perilous position that invited aggression before June 5, 1967, and her promise to forego "further expansionist aims," the report proposes that:

> "Second, the Arab governments must declare their acceptance of the fact of Israel's existence as a sovereign state and must make clear their willingness to live in a condition of true peace with Israel." (p. 96)

In contrast to the specific demand made on Israel for giving up territory and abandoning its goal of secure, defensible borders, the Arab governments are not required to make any substantive commitment whatever. They are not asked to recognize Israel in a formal, diplomatic sense; nor is any rigor attached to the requirement that they "make clear their willingness to live in a condition of true peace with Israel." How, one might ask the Quaker authors, should that "willingness" be made clear?

Of course, recognition of the sovereign rights of Israel and willingness to refrain from threats or acts of war—more, in fact, than the Quakers demand from the Arab states—are incumbent on every member state of the United Nations as clearly specified in Article 2 of the U.N. Charter. Thus, the Arab states would be rewarded by the Quaker authors merely for accepting their basic U.N. obligations after violating them for twenty years.

Since the report asks the Arabs to "declare their acceptance" of

Israel's existence as a sovereign state and to make clear their willingness to live in peace with Israel, why do the authors persist in refusing to call for direct negotiations between the two sides? If Arab acceptance of Israel's sovereign rights and Arab willingness to live in peace with Israel are to have real meaning and carry conviction, what better way to start than by direct, face-to-face negotiations which would serve both as evidence of the new order of things in the Middle East and as the best method of achieving a final, binding and freely negotiated settlement of all outstanding differences? But the Quaker report never asks the Arab states for such a genuine commitment to eventual peace. They are willing to settle merely for Arab "acceptance" of the facts of life and a "willingness" to live in peace with those facts.

As the historical record makes clear, beginning with the U.N. Partition Plan of 1947, the Arab states have shown little regard for either international law in general or their own solemn commitments in particular. They have reneged even on agreements to which they had freely committed themselves. This was especially and repeatedly true, for example, in the case of Sharm el Sheikh and the Straits of Tiran, the use of the Suez Canal, the demilitarization of the Golan Heights, the demilitarization of the Gaza Strip, the right of free access to the religious shrines of the Old City of Jerusalem and to the Western Wall, and many more. Egypt's unilateral abrogation in 1969 of the U.N. cease-fire which ended the Six-Day War in 1967 was followed in August 1970 by a blatant violation of the terms of the new cease-fire, promoted under U.S. auspices, when the Russians and Egyptians jointly moved their missiles into the "standstill" zone along the Suez Canal.

Against this history of broken pledges and agreements, and after three costly wars and unremitting Arab efforts to destroy her, Israel is required by the Quaker authors to forego the possibility of negotiating a real peace, with secure and agreed borders, and rely instead on Arab "willingness" to live in peace. Moreover, once Israel has committed herself as a first step to withdraw from all the occupied territory, as the report proposes, what would she have left to negotiate with in the next phase? Since the Arabs will have been assured the return of the lost territory, what need or incentive would they have to carry forward good-faith negotiations on the other important issues which threaten peace and stability in the Middle East?

The Quakers' *Search for Peace in the Middle East* next proposes that:

> "Third, the Big Four should declare their readiness to underwrite a peace settlement agreed upon by Israel, Jordan and Egypt and negotiated in consultation with the Palestinian Arabs." (p. 96)

This step need not detain us too long. Of the Big Four, the U.S.S.R. is a formal ally of Egypt; France has made no secret of its partisan support for the Arab cause; the United Kingdom, with traditional British restraint, has not been quite so open about it but its sensitivities toward Arab oil interests are traditional; and the United States, despite the report's assertions to the contrary, has never been simply pro-Israel. The commitment of the U.S.S.R. to Egypt, for example, is of an entirely different nature and order of intensity and magnitude than U.S. support for Israel. Given the realities of Big Four global and economic concerns, any suggestion of their corporate impartiality is a patent travesty of the truth.

Three of the Big Four—the U.S., France and Great Britain—had in fact underwritten the solemn declaration of the world's maritime powers on the principle of free navigation through the Straits of Tiran in 1957. These undertakings turned out to be worthless in 1967.

There is no reason to expect that the Big Four could or would guarantee a true peace in the Middle East. The Soviets, for example, have an enormous investment in the continuation of a no-peace-no-war state of tension. True peace would reduce their leverage with the Arab states to a point inimical to their ambitions in the Middle East, Asia and Africa. France and Great Britain, from their own public records, are mainly concerned with shoring up what is left of their influence among the Arab states and extending their economic ties with the oil-producing states. The U.S. does have a real interest in promoting a stable peace in the area as the best hope for restoring its influence among the Arab states, but for its own economic and political reasons it is unwilling to risk offending the Arab states by insisting on the processes and substance which are essential to a permanent solution.

Since there is no discernible reason to expect the Big Four to forego their own interests and act altruistically, the report's emphasis on Big Four participation appears to be based primarily on their power to shape a "settlement" and enforce it—a concept grossly inconsistent with the usual Quaker espousal of the rights of small countries.

What the Quaker authors are advocating is a reconstruction of the situation in the Middle East that existed on June 4, 1967. For those interested in true and lasting peace, this is a dangerous prescription. In the end, the recommendations in *Search for Peace in the Middle East* turn out to be nothing more than still another attempt to have the major powers settle the fate of smaller nations. The idea of insisting that the parties to the conflict themselves be the parties to the peace is rejected out of hand.

This is so despite the report's use of the words "agreed upon" in reference to a peace settlement. The Quaker authors do not propose that the Arabs and Israel negotiate the terms of the peace settlement but only "agree" to them. Similarly, with respect to negotiations "in consultation with the Palestinian Arabs," the report does not indicate who really represents the Palestinians, and by what right; nor does it explain how any negotiations are to take place "in consultation" with them. In short, the whole proposal seems to have little touch with reality.

*The Second Step*

In pursuit of military disengagement, the Quakers make a set of second-step proposals which involve a "substantial United Nations emergency peace-keeping force"; a special U.N. Commission to supervise the cease-fire and to compile "an accurate and immediate record of all acts of violence, whether labeled as terrorism or counter-terrorism"; and a U.N.-convened conference to explore "ways of reducing the flow of arms into the Middle East and to undertake suitable U.N. action declaring the Middle East a nuclear-free zone." (p. 97)

To anyone at all familiar with the recent history of the Middle East, and particularly with the experience of U.N. agencies and forces, this whole approach must evoke memories of Alice in Wonderland. The authors seem determined to persist in assigning responsibilities to the U.N. which it has repeatedly proven incapable of fulfilling. They avoid the complicated reality of Big Power conflicts and U.N. politics and disregard the whole unhappy history of the U.N. Security Council, especially as it applies to the Middle East. Rather, they seem to be asking the nations of the

Middle East, and the world, to place their confidence once again in the same defective arrangements that have already failed three times before.

Further, given the rigid anti-Israel voting pattern in the U.N. of the Arab, Moslem and Soviet-bloc countries, to say nothing of the Afro-Asian nations and France; the fact that 36 member states refuse to have diplomatic relations with Israel; and the Soviet's uninhibited use of its veto power in the Security Council, the Quaker authors' willingness to place all of Israel's eggs in the U.N. basket represents at best a measure of wishful thinking that can be far more dangerous than the situation it purports to resolve. To be of such short memory, in this instance, is more sinful than to be of little faith.

*The Third Step*

The report's third step toward peace presents "guidelines" for structuring "a political settlement." The details of these guidelines follow quite naturally from the first and second steps toward a "practical peace settlement." The most important provisions involve the following:

1) The right of existence of all states in the Middle East must be accepted by all other states in the area, and all claims and acts of belligerency must be ended.
2) Israel must abandon all "claims to the acquisition of territory by conquest in the June War of 1967" and make firm commitments for withdrawal from those territories.
3) All parties must recognize the right of self-determination for the Palestinians. Pending such a determination a temporary U.N. Trusteeship or "some comparable type of international administration" will replace the Israeli military occupation of Gaza and the West Bank.
4) Jerusalem should be united, but not under Israeli control; rather, in time it "should be possible to create some sort of Federal condominium"; meanwhile, separate Arab and Jewish boroughs under "some coordinating United Nations agency" would be most satisfactory.
5) The Arab refugees should have the choice, "within some agreed annual maximum," of repatriation or compensation for their loss of properties and relocation.

6) Free and innocent passage of the shipping of all nations must be guaranteed through the Gulf of Aqaba and the Suez Canal.

In essence, the report finally reaches the point of advocating nothing more or less than re-establishment of the situation envisaged by the 1947 U.N. Partition Plan—22 years and three wars later. Here too the authors' conclusions seem to have distorted the past history and current situation on which the recommendations are presumably based. Even more disturbing, however, is the fact that they implicitly recognize, although they refuse to acknowledge, the extreme danger to Israel's survival embodied in their proposals.

In this connection, we note that even at this third stage in their approach the authors maintain that a comprehensive peace plan cannot be achieved. "Certainly this is quite impossible in the form of bilateral 'direct negotiations' for which the Israelis have so persistently pressed." (p. 98)

The report goes on to describe the need for further and extended Big Power, U.N. and "other" involvements although "eventually, under United Nations auspices, representatives of the Arabs, specifically including the Palestinians, and of the Israelis, must accept concrete agreements . . . encased in official, public, written documents." (p. 98)

Thus, while Israel returns to her pre-war borders, surrenders control of her capital city of Jerusalem, offers repatriation to an undefined number of Palestinian Arabs and contributes to the compensation of those who do not return, the Arabs are not even asked to show good faith by negotiating the details directly and signing a final, binding peace treaty.

Instead, the Arab states are insulated from the need to face the Israelis directly and thus effectively recognize Israel's sovereign status. They are asked "eventually" to only accept "official, public written documents" but not a treaty of peace.

These, unhappily, are not mere issues of semantics. The Quaker authors quite obviously (as admitted later by Dr. Bolling) recognized that the basic issue in the Arab-Israeli conflict is not over territory—the Israelis have never asked more than "secure and agreed" borders; nor is it over the refugees—the Arab states launched their first war against Israel in 1947-48, before there were any refugees, and subsequently exploited the Arab refugees for their own internal and international purposes, having denied them both the opportunity for resettlement and the right of self-determination.

The real issue, complicated by other historical forces at work in the Middle East, is the unremitting hostility of the Arab states towards the existence of Israel. An honest search for peace would have admitted that fact and worked toward its reduction.

CHAPTER X

# ADVICE TO AMERICAN JEWS

In addition to repeated strictures to the "American Jewish establishment" for its alleged identification with "hard-line" elements within the Israeli government, the Quaker authors have some further advice to American Jews. It is instructive in this connection to study the text of the twelfth draft of the Quaker report:

> "We appeal to the leaders of the powerful American Jewish community, whose hard work and generous financial support have been so important to the building and sustaining of Israel, to reassess the character of their support and the nature of their role in American politics. Our impression, confirmed by many comments from Israelis inside Israel, is that there is a tendency for the leaders of the American Jewish establishment to identify themselves with the more hard-line elements inside the Israeli cabinet, 'to out-hawk the hawks,' and to ignore or discount the dissident elements, in and out of the Israeli Government, that are searching for more creative ways to solve the Middle East problems.
>
> "As free American citizens, members of the American Jewish community have every right to utilize all the instruments of a free society to register their convictions and desires, and to try to influence legislative and executive action. However, the heavy-handed nature of some of these pressures and their extensiveness have served to inhibit calm and rational public discussion of the issues in the Arab-Israeli conflict. It is not a new phenomenon in American politics, but it is nonetheless disturbing to have Congressmen complain privately that they have signed public statements giving unqualified endorsement for Israel, even though they do not believe in those statements, or have agreed to sponsor resolutions concerning American policy toward Israel of which they secretly disapprove—simply because they are intimidated by Jewish pressure groups. In this situation are clear dangers of an anti-Semitic backlash. No one who is truly concerned about the long-term fate of Israel and the long-term threats to interfaith harmony and brotherhood can be indifferent to those dangers." (pp. 52-53)

Putting aside the many questions of fact which these allegations raise, their evocative phraseology is worth noting:

> ". . . leaders of the *powerful* American Jewish community . . . [should] reassess the *character* of their support and the *nature* of their role in American politics. . . . [They] *'out-hawk the hawks'* . . . ignore or discount more *creative ways*. . . . The *heavy-handed nature* of [their] pressures . . . *inhibit calm and rational* public discussions. . . . *Congressmen complain privately* . . . because they are *intimidated by Jewish pressure groups*. . . . *Clear dangers of an anti-Semitic backlash* [and] threats to *the long-term fate of Israel* . . . and . . . to interfaith *harmony* and *brotherhood* . . ."

Stripped of its pious verbal camouflage, this statement can only be described as threatening American Jews that unless they cut back in their efforts "to register their convictions and desires" as regards "legislative and executive action," they may face an "anti-Semitic backlash"—with all this connotes for the future of Israel and American Jewry. Regardless of motive, the fact that the Quaker authors urge American Jews to limit the exercise of their constitutional rights or face potentially dangerous results clearly implies that American Jews are something less than first-class American citizens. If they are to be subject to "anti-Semitic backlash" when their efforts, though legal and orderly, exceed the authors' norms for propriety, then Jews are being set aside as a special class whose rights "as free American citizens" are effectively limited by the censorship of the non-Jewish majority.

This is especially strange and dangerous advice coming from the Quakers, themselves a religious minority, who practice freely so many highly visible forms of civil disobedience in registering their "convictions and desires." Readers of the twelfth draft—among them a group of professors from Harvard University who met with some members of the Quaker group early in 1970—observed that "anti-Semitic backlash" might already be showing itself in the authors' own treatment of the issue. In later drafts this section was altered to read as follows:

> "We appeal to the leaders of the American Jewish Community, whose hard work and generous financial support have been so important to the building and sustaining of Israel, to reassess the ways in which their support can further the cause of peace and security for Israel and to re-examine the full implications of their role with

> respect to American Middle East policies. Our impression, confirmed by many comments from Israelis inside Israel, is that there is a tendency for some of the leaders of the American Jewish establishment to identify themselves with the more hard-line elements inside the Israeli cabinet and to ignore or discount the dissident elements, in and out of the Israeli government, that are searching for more creative ways to solve the Middle East problems.
>
> "As American Jews, most of whom have a strong sense of identity with Israel, search for ways to express their concern and support, we urge them to make special efforts to explore the variety of options available for peace in the Middle East, to reject simplistic military solutions, and to encourage calm and deliberate examination of all the issues. The same admonitions, of course, apply to all other groups which attempt to influence public opinion and government action toward the Middle East." (pp. 116-117)

While this language is considerably more felicitous, most of the inferences are still there, recalling the earlier, less inhibited statement of advice. The advice to American Jews "to re-examine the full implications of their role with respect to American Middle East policies," still warns American Jews to be wary of exercising their rights as citizens.

Although the authors may have been motivated only by a friendly desire to warn the Jewish community about the potential danger of anti-Semitic backlash, their use of such evocative phrases in the twelfth draft and the persistent tone of their advice in the final draft indicate (at the least) a regrettable lack of sensitivity.

(It may be noted parenthetically that when the Quaker authors met with the Harvard professors in early 1970 they were pressed to document their charge that "Congressmen complain privately . . . that they are intimidated by Jewish pressure groups." They first parried the question and finally could recall only one such alleged complaint, from a congressman whose constituency was virtually free of Jews.)

CHAPTER XI

# THE QUAKER ATTEMPT AT INTERVENTION

Along with a great number of expressions of noble sentiment and disclaimers of any special interest, the Quaker report attempts to insulate itself from criticism by the style and tone which it uses so effectively. Essentially, it eschews inflammatory rhetoric and relies on bland, "even-handed" observations. Inconvenient facts are innocently omitted, however essential such facts might be to an understanding of the issues.

Whole sections of pertinent historical facts are simply left out where their inclusion would have threatened or destroyed the authors' thesis. Thus, the section on "Background" distorts, by omission alone, the whole complex of events that led to the establishment of the State of Israel and the wars of 1948, 1956–57 and 1967. The result is a "background" tailored to meet the requirements of the authors' pre-determined conclusions.

Also, major statements are casually made, with no evidence offered in support, on the apparent assumption that they should be accepted without question merely because they were advanced by men of apparent probity and disinterestedness. Finally, the body of the report draws conclusions without basis even in the material presented by the authors. And it is full of "factual" data tending solely to prejudice the reader against Israel.

As we have seen, for example, the authors reserve their pejoratives solely for the policies, actions and structure of the Israeli government, and for Israel's Jewish supporters in the U.S. There is not a single word of comparable criticism of any Arab government, Arab terrorists or the Soviet Union.

In sum, we find that the Quakers' *Search for Peace in the Middle East,* from its earliest drafts to the final published version, betrays a pre-determined bias, rationalized by historical distortion, that is harmful to the cause of a just and lasting peace.

Nevertheless, in discussing their role, the authors of the report frequently cite the fact that their views have been attacked by both Arabs and Jews as a sign that they are on the right track—that because they are neutral intercessors they may be able to persuade both sides to bridge their differences. But in order to be effective, mediators must be acceptable to and trusted by both sides. Especially when they are self-appointed, as in this case, they are not likely to be successful if they are seen as biased and inaccurate by either side.

The Quaker attempt at intervention in the Arab-Israeli conflict has added to the burden imposed on both sides by the interference of third parties intent on using the conflict to achieve their own goals. Certainly the cumulative effect of the series of contacts with the Quaker authors has been to arouse great hostility toward them among Jews. The dismissal by the authors of the comments on the various drafts by Jewish scholars precludes their ever being acceptable as intercessors; it also endangers the previous good relationship between Jews and the Quaker community, which appears to be sponsoring this anti-Israel intervention. The current state of affairs is particularly regrettable because of the long history of mutual respect and sympathy between American Jews and American Friends and their past collaboration in many humanitarian causes.

We believe that the great body of the Quaker movement seeks only truth and fairness in its approach to any issue and would reject any "slant" imposed on the facts for any reason. Hence we address this critique also to Quakers themselves. We ask them to review the contents of the report in the light of their own consciences and critical faculties.

In the same spirit, we suggest that the facts and analysis which form the substance of our critique may challenge other well-intentioned readers to re-examine the basis of their own views and opinions about Israel. Certainly the Quaker report group has not been unique in allowing bias and historical distortion, conscious or unconscious, to interfere with a rational understanding of the Arab-Israeli dilemma. Christians who purport to seek only reasonable discourse often accuse Jews of hypersensitivity on the issue of Israel. Yet unhappy experience indicates that, in far too many cases, the underlying difficulty is not related to questions of objective fact or the inherent problems of dispassionate analysis.

Since overt anti-Semitism is no longer acceptable among thinking people of any persuasion, anti-Zionism has proven a convenient, if not convincing substitute. Zionism, it should be realized, is a movement of Jewish national renaissance. It cannot be separated from authentic Jewishness because it embodies Judaism's prophetic vision of justice and peace; its affirmation is at the core of the spiritual and cultural identity of the Jewish people.

One of the more tragic aspects of the problem, often reflected in frustrated attempts at constructive dialogue, is that many of the critics of both Israel and its Jewish supporters appear quite unaware of the possibility of their own unconscious prejudice. Even in an age where the spirit of ecumenism and interfaith goodwill have gained new importance, the remarkable force of "theological anti-Semitism" has shown itself in recent years. The basic attitude of some Christians, theologians as well as laymen, is still deeply rooted in the postulate that because the Jews refused to accept Jesus as the Messiah, they are eternally damned and condemned to wander the earth as homeless witnesses to their sin. We believe that by far the largest part of this new evocation of anti-Semitism goes unrecognized because it is *not* conscious.

On the other hand, the tragedy of the past two thousand years of Jewish history has made Jews highly sensitive to the issue of Jewish survival and renaissance—and that issue, for them, is now inextricably bound up with the issue of Israel's survival as a free and independent state. Most non-Jews, although they may have deep concern about the people and affairs of the Middle East, are spared the intense sense of urgency which informs Jewish sensitivity on the subject.

In a world as complex and uncertain as ours, there remains ample room for criticism of the policies and actions of any nation, people or individuals, including Israel and the Jews. Such criticism, of course, is best judged in terms of the objective facts and historical circumstances. This responsibility is no less incumbent on Israel's supporters than on her critics.

It is our hope, therefore, that even beyond the immediate issues of the Quaker report, our critique may contribute both to a more accurate assessment of the Middle East crisis and to the future of meaningful interfaith dialogue.

The search for peace in the Middle East, of course, must go forward. But the tragedy of this Quaker group's self-generated intercession is that the search for peace will now carry the unnecessary burden of another false and biased account of the problem, and a misguided prescription for its solution.

# BIBLIOGRAPHY


American Academic Association for Peace in the Middle East, *The Anatomy of Peace in the Middle East.* Proceedings of the Annual Conference, 1969.

American Professors for Peace in the Middle East (Boston Chapter), *U.S. Middle East Policy: Peace or Appeasement,* 1970.

Azcarate y Florez, Pablo de, *Mission in Palestine, 1948-1952.* Washington, D.C.: Middle East Institute, 1966.

Bar-Zohar, Michael, *Embassies in Crisis.* New Jersey: Prentice-Hall, 1970.

Crossman, Richard H. S., *Palestine Mission, a personal record.* New York: Harper, 1947.

Crum, Bartley C., *Behind the Silken Curtain.* New York: Simon & Schuster, 1947.

Dagan, Avigdor, *Moscow and Jerusalem.* London: Abelard-Schuman, 1970.

Dayan, Moshe, *Diary of the Sinai Campaign.* New York: Harper and Row, 1966.

Draper, Theodore, *Israel and World Politics: Roots of the Third Arab-Israeli War.* New York: Viking Press, 1968.

Eckhardt, A. Roy, *Elder and Younger Brothers: The Encounter of Jews and Christians.* (See especially the appendix which consists of two articles by A. Roy and Alice L. Eckhardt in *The Christian Century,* July 26 and August 2, 1967). New York: Charles Scribner's Sons, 1967.

Esco Foundation for Palestine, *Palestine: A Study of Jewish, Arab and British Policies, 2 Volumes.* New Haven: Yale University Press, 1947.

Eytan, Walter, *The First Ten Years: A Diplomatic History of Israel.* New York: Simon and Schuster, 1958.

Feingold, Henry L., *The Politics of Rescue: The Roosevelt Administration and the Holocaust, 1938-1945. New Brunswick:* Rutgers University Press.

Feis, Herbert, *The Birth of Israel.* New York: Norton, 1969.

Finer, Herman, *Dulles Over Suez.* Chicago: Quadrangle Books, 1964.

Flannery, Edward H., *The Anguish of the Jews: Twenty-Three Centuries of Anti-Semitism.* New York: Macmillan, 1965.

Garcia Granados, Jorge, *The Birth of Israel: The Drama as I Saw It.* New York: Knopf, 1949.

Goitein, Shlomo D., *Jews and Arabs: Their Contacts Through the Ages.* New York: Schocken Books, 1964.

Halpern, Ben., *The Idea of the Jewish State.* Cambridge, Mass.: Harvard University Press, 1969.

Hertzberg, Arthur, *The Zionist Idea: A Historical Analysis & Reader.* New York: Atheneum (and JPS), 1970.

Hurewitz, Jacob C., *The Struggle for Palestine.* New York: Greenwood Press, 1968.

Kaplan, Deborah, *The Arab Refugees.* Jerusalem: Reuben Mass, 1959.

Kimche, David and Bawly, Dan. *The Sandstorm: The Arab-Israeli War of June 1967—Prelude and Aftermath.* New York: Stein and Day, 1968.

Kurzman, Dan, *Genesis 1948: The First Arab-Israeli War.* Cleveland: World Publishing Co., 1970.

Lall, Arthur, *The UN and the Middle East Crisis, 1967.* New York: Columbia University Press, 1968.

Laqueur, Walter, *The Israel-Arab Reader.* New York: Citadel Press, 1968; *The Road to Jerusalem.* New York: Macmillan Co., 1968; *The Struggle for the Middle East.* New York: Macmillan Co., 1969.

Lewis, Bernard (testimony of), Hearings before the Subcommittee on National Security and International Operations of the Committee on Government Operations, U.S. Senate—part 4, March 17, 1971. Washington: U.S. Govt. Printing Office, 1971.

McDonald, James G., *My Mission in Israel, 1948-1951.* New York: Simon and Schuster, 1951.

Parkes, James, *Whose Land? A History of the Peoples of Palestine.* New York: Taplinger, 1971.

Prittie, Terence, *Israel: Miracle in the Desert.* Baltimore: Penguin Books, 1968.

Ra'anan, Uri, *The USSR Arms the Third World.* Cambridge, Mass.: MIT Press, 1969.

Schapiro, Leonard (testimony of), Hearings before the Subcommittee on National Security and International Operations of the Committee on Government Operations, U.S. Senate—part 2, April 16, 1970. Washington: U.S. Govt. Printing Office, 1970.

Schechtman, Joseph B. *On Wings of Eagles: The Plight, Exodus, and Homecoming of Oriental Jewry.* New York: T. Yoseloff, 1961.

Schechtman, Joseph, *The Arab Refugee Problem.* New York: Philosophical Library, 1952.

Soustelle, Jacques, *The Long March of Israel.* New York: American Heritage Press, 1969.

Stein, Leonard, *The Balfour Declaration.* New York: Simon and Schuster, 1961.

Stock, Ernest, *Israel on the Road to Sinai, 1949-1956, with a Sequel on the Six-Day War, 1967*. Ithaca, New York: Cornell University Press, 1967.

Stock, Ernest, *From Conflict to Understanding: Relations between Jews and Arabs in Israel since 1948*. New York: Institute of Human Relations Press, 1968.

Stone, Julius, *Self-Determination and the Palestinian Arabs*. (Paper presented to the Australian Society of Legal Philosophy and the Grotian Society). Truman Research Institute, Jerusalem, 1970.

Sykes, Christopher, *Crossroads to Israel*. Cleveland, Ohio: World Publishing Co., 1965.

Teveth, Shebtai, *The Cursed Blessing: The Story of Israel's Occupation of the West Bank*. New York: Random House, 1970.

## Appendix I

# LAND OWNERSHIP IN PALESTINE 1880-1948

by MOSHE AUMANN

A great deal has been spoken and written over the years on the subject of land ownership in Israel—or, before 1948, Palestine. Arab propaganda, in particular, has been at pains to convince the world, with the aid of copious statistics, that the Arabs "own" Palestine, morally and legally, and that whatever Jewish land ownership there may be is negligible. From this conclusions have been drawn (or implied) with regard to the sovereign rights of the State of Israel and the problem of the Arab refugees.

The Arab case against Israel, in the matter of Jewish land purchases, rests mainly on two claims: (1) that the Palestinian Arab farmer was peacefully and contentedly working his land in the latter part of the 19th century and the early part of the 20th when along came the European Jewish immigrant, drove him off his land, disrupted the normal development of the country and created a vast class of landless, dispossessed Arabs; (2) that a small Jewish minority, owning an even smaller proportion of Palestinian lands (5 percent as against the Arabs' 95 percent), illegally made itself master of Palestine in 1948.

Our purpose in this pamphlet is to set the record straight by marshalling the facts and figures pertaining to this very complex subject, on the basis of the most reliable and authoritative information available, and to trace the history of modern Jewish resettlement purely from the point of view of the sale and purchase of land.

### *Pre-1948 Conditions in Palestine*

A study of Palestine under Turkish rule reveals that already at the beginning of the 18th century, long before Jewish land purchases and large-scale Jewish immigration started, the position of the Palestinian fellah (peasant) had begun to deteriorate. The heavy burden of taxation, coming on top of chronic indebtedness to money-lenders, drove a growing number of farmers to place themselves under the protection of men of wealth or of the Moslem religious endowment fund (*Waqf*), with the result that they were eventually compelled to give up their title to the land, if not their actual residence upon and cultivation of it.

Until the passage of the Turkish Land Registry Law in 1858, there were no official deeds to attest to a man's legal title to a parcel of land; tradition alone had to suffice to establish such title—and usually it did. And yet, the position of Palestine's farmers was a precarious one, for there were constant blood-feuds between families, clans and entire villages, as well as periodic incursions by rapacious Bedouin tribes, such as the notorious Ben Sakk'r, of whom H.B. Tristram (*The Land of Israel: A Journal of Travels in Palestine,* Society for Promoting Christian Knowledge, London, 1865) wrote that they "can muster 1,000 cavalry and always join their brethren when a raid or war is on the move. They have obtained their present possessions gradually and, in great measure, by driving out the fellahin (peasants), destroying their villages and reducing their rich corn-fields to pasturage." (p. 488)

Tristram goes on to present a remarkable and highly revealing description of conditions in Palestine on both sides of the Jordan River in the middle of the 19th century—a description that belies the Arab claim of a tranquil, normally developing Palestinian rural economy allegedly disrupted by Jewish immigration and settlement.

> A few years ago, the whole Ghor was in the hands of the fellahin, and much of it cultivated for corn. Now the whole of it is in the hands of the Bedouin, who eschew all agriculture, except in a few spots cultivated here and there by their slaves; and with the Bedouin come lawlessness and the uprooting of all Turkish authority. No government is now acknowledged on the east side; and unless the Porte acts with greater firmness and caution than is his wont . . . Palestine will be desolated and given up to the nomads.
> The same thing is now going on over the plain of Sharon, where, both in the north and south, land is going out of cultivation, and whole villages rapidly disappearing from the face of the earth. Since the year 1838, no less than 20 villages have been thus erased from the map and the stationary population extirpated. Very rapidly the Bedouin are encroaching wherever horse can be ridden; and the Government is utterly powerless to resist them or to defend its subjects. (p. 490)

For descriptions of other parts of the country, we are indebted to the 1937 Report of the Palestine Royal Commission—though, for lack of space, we can quote but the briefest passages. In Chapter 9, para. 43 the Report quotes an eye-witness account of the condition of the Maritime Plain in 1913:

> The road leading from Gaza to the north was only a summer track suitable for transport by camels and carts . . . no orange groves, orchards or vineyards were to be seen until one reached Yabna village. . . . Not in a single village in all this area was water used for irrigation. . . . Houses were all of mud. No windows were anywhere to be seen. . . . The ploughs used were of wood. . . . The yields were very poor. . . . The sanitary conditions in the village were horrible. Schools did not

> exist. . . . The rate of infant mortality was very high. . . .
> The area north of Jaffa . . . consisted of two distinctive parts. . . . The eastern part, in the direction of the hills, resembled in culture that of the Gaza-Jaffa area. . . . The western part, towards the sea, was almost a desert. . . . The villages in this area were few and thinly populated. Many ruins of villages were scattered over the area, as owing to the prevalence of malaria, many villages were deserted by their inhabitants.

The Huleh basin, below the Syrian border, is described as "including a number of Arab villages and a large papyrus swamp draining south into Lake Huleh . . . a triangular strip of land some 44 sq. miles in area. . . . This tract is irrigated in a very haphazard manner by a network of small, primitive canals. It is, owing to over-irrigation, now the most malarious tract in all Palestine. It might become one of the most fertile."

With regard to yet another region in Palestine—the Beisan (Beit Shean) area—we quote from the report of Mr. Lewis French, Director of Development appointed by the British Government in 1931:

> We found it inhabited by fellahin who lived in mud hovels and suffered severely from the prevalent malaria. . . . Large areas of their lands were uncultivated and covered with weeds. There were no trees, no vegetables. The fellahin, if not themselves cattle thieves, were always ready to harbour these and other criminals. The individual plots of cultivation changed hands annually. There was little public security, and the fellahin's lot was an alternation of pillage and blackmail by their neighbours the Bedouin.

This, then, was the picture of Palestine in the closing decades of the 19th century and up to the First World War: a land that was overwhelmingly desert, with nomads continually encroaching on the settled areas and its farmers; a lack of elementary facilities and equipment; peasants wallowing in poverty, ignorance and disease, saddled with debts (interest rates at times were as high as 60 percent) and threatened by warlike nomads or neighboring clans. The result was a growing neglect of the soil and a flight from the villages, with a mounting concentration of lands in the hands of a small number of large landowners, frequently residing in such distant Arab capitals as Beirut and Damascus, Cairo and Kuwait. Here, in other words, was a social and economic order that had all the earmarks of a medieval feudal society.

### *Who Dispossessed the Palestinian Peasant?*

The Palestinian peasant was indeed being dispossessed, but by his fellow-Arabs: the local sheikh and village elders, the Government tax-collector, the merchants and money-lenders; and, when he was a tenant-farmer (as was usually the case), by the absentee-owner. By the time the season's crop had been distributed among all these, little if anything remained for him and his family, and new debts generally had to be incurred to pay off the old. Then the Bedouin came along and took their "cut," or drove the hapless fellah off the land altogether.

This was the "normal" course of events in 19th century Palestine. It was disrupted by the advent of the Jewish pioneering enterprise, which sounded the death-knell of this medieval feudal system. In this way the Jews played an objective revolutionary role. Small wonder that it aroused the ire and active opposition of the Arab sheikhs, absentee landowners, money-lenders and Bedouin bandits.

*Jewish Land Purchases*

It is important to note that the first enduring Jewish agricultural settlement in modern Palestine was founded not by European refugees, but by a group of old-time families leaving the overcrowded Jewish Quarter of the Old City of Jerusalem. (According to the Turkish census of 1875, by that time Jews already constituted a majority of the population of Jerusalem and by 1905 comprised two-thirds of its citizens. The *Encyclopaedia Britannica* of 1910 gives the population figure as 60,000, of whom 40,000 were Jews.)

In 1878 they founded the village of Petah Tikva in the Sharon Plain —a village that was to become known as the "Mother of Jewish Settlements" in Palestine. Four years later a group of pioneering immigrants from Russia settled in Rishon le-Zion. Other farming villages followed in rapid succession.

When considering Jewish land purchases and settlement, four factors should be borne in mind:

(1) Most of the land purchases involved large tracts belonging to absentee owners. (Virtually all of the Jezreel Valley, for example, belonged in 1897 to only two persons: the eastern portion to the Turkish Sultan, and the western part to the richest banker in Syria, Sursuk "the Greek.")

(2) Most of the land purchased had not been cultivated previously because it was swampy, rocky, sandy or, for some other reason, regarded as uncultivable. This is supported by the findings of the Peel Commission Report (p. 242): "The Arab charge that the Jews have obtained too large a proportion of good land cannot be maintained. Much of the land now carrying orange groves was sand dunes or swamp and uncultivated when it was purchased . . . there was at the time at least of the earlier sales little evidence that the owners possessed either the resources or training needed to develop the land." (1937)

(3) While, for this reason, the early transactions did not involve unduly large sums of money, the price of land began to rise as Arab landowners took advantage of the growing demand for rural tracts. The

resulting infusion of capital into the Palestinian economy had noticeable beneficial effects on the standard of living of all the inhabitants.

(4) The Jewish pioneers introduced new farming methods which improved the soil and crop cultivation and were soon emulated by Arab farmers.

The following figures show land purchases by the three leading Jewish land-buying organizations and by individual Jews between 1880 and 1935.

JEWISH LAND PURCHASES, 1880–1935 (in dunams*)

| *Organization* | *Total land acquired* | *Government conces-sions* | *From private owners* | *Large tracts*** | |
|---|---|---|---|---|---|
| | | | | *Dunams* | *Percent (approx.)* |
| PICA (Palestine Jewish Colonization Assoc.) | 469,407 | 39,520 | 429,887 | 293,545 | 70 |
| Palestine Land Development Co. | 579,492 | 66,513*** | 512,979 | 455,169 | 90 |
| Jewish National Fund**** | 836,396 | | | | |
| Until 1930 | | | 270,084 | 239,170 | 90 |
| 1931–1947 | | | 566,312 | | 50 |
| Individual Jews | 432,100 | | 432,100 | | 50 |

* 4 dunams = 1 acre.

** The large tracts often belonged to absentee landlords.

*** Land situated in the sandy Beersheba and marshy Huleh districts.

**** ". . . created on December 25, 1901, to ensure that land would be purchased for the Jewish workers who were to be personally responsible for its cultivation.

"Since the J.N.F. was as concerned with conforming to socialist ideals as with intensive economic exploitation of land, its Charter was opposed to the use of lands purchased by it as private property. The J.N.F. retained the freehold of the lands, while the people working it are only life tenants. . . .

"The capital of the Jewish National Fund was essentially raised from small regular donations from millions of Jewish craftsmen, labourers, shopowners and intellectuals in Central and Eastern Europe where the shadow of genocide was already apparent, who felt concerned about the return of Jews to Zion. . . .

"Contrary to colonialist enterprises, which were seeking an exorbitant profit from land extorted from the colonized peoples, Zionist settlement discouraged private capital as its enterprise was of a socialist nature based on the refusal to exploit the worker." (Kurt Niedermaier, *Colonisation Without Colonialism,* Youth and Hechalutz Dept., Jewish Agency, Jerusalem, 1969).

From the above table it will be seen that the proportion of land purchased from large (usually absentee) owners ranged from about 50 to 90 percent.

"The total area of land in Jewish possession at the end of June 1947," writes A. Granott in *The Land System in Palestine* (Eyre and Spottiswoode, London, 1952, p. 278), "amounted to 1,850,000 dunams; of this, 181,100 dunams had been obtained through concessions from the Palestine Government, and about 120,000 dunams had been acquired from Churches, from foreign companies, from the Government otherwise than by concessions, and so forth. It was estimated that 1,000,000 dunams and more, or 57 percent, had been acquired from large Arab landowners, and if to this we add the lands acquired from the Government, Churches, and foreign companies, the percentage will amount to seventy-three. From the fellaheen there had been purchased about 500,000 dunams, or 27 percent, of the total area acquired. The result of Jewish land acquisitions, at least to a considerable part, was that properties which had been in the hands of large and medium owners were converted into holdings of small peasants."

*The League of Nations Mandate*

When the League of Nations conferred the Mandate for Palestine upon Great Britain in 1922, it expressly stipulated that "The Administration of Palestine . . . shall encourage, in cooperation with the Jewish Agency . . . close settlement by Jews on the land, including State lands and waste lands not acquired for public purposes" (Article 6), and that it "shall introduce a land system appropriate to the needs of the country, having regard, among other things, to the desirability of promoting the close settlement and intensive cultivation of the land." (Article 11)

British policy, however, followed a different course, deferring to the extremist Arab opposition to the above-mentioned provision of the Mandate. Of some 750,000 dunams of cultivable State lands, 350,000, or nearly half, had been allotted by 1949 to Arabs and only 17,000 dunams to Jews. This was in clear violation of the terms of the Mandate. Nor, ironically enough, did it help the Arab peasants for whose benefit these transactions were ostensibly carried out. The glaring examples of this policy are the case of the Beisan lands and that of the Huleh Concession.

*Beisan Lands*

Under the Ghor-Mudawwarra Agreement of 1921, some 225,000 dunams of potentially fertile wasteland in the Beisan (Beit Shean) area were handed over to Arab farmers on terms severely condemned not only by Jews but also by such British experts as Lewis French and Sir John Hope-Simpson. More than half of the land was irrigable, and, according to the British experts, eight dunams of irrigated land per capita (or 50–60 dunams per family) were sufficient to enable a family to maintain itself on the land. Yet many farmers received far more than that: six families, of whom two lived in Syria, received a combined area of about 7,000 dunams; four families (some living in Egypt) received a combined area of 3,496 dunams; another received 3,450 and yet another, 1,350.

Thus the Ghor-Mudawwarra Agreement was instrumental in creating a new group of large landowners. Possessing huge tracts, most of which they were unable to till, these owners began to sell the surplus lands at speculative prices. In his 1930 Report, Sir Hope-Simpson wrote of the Agreement that it had deprived the Government of "the control of a large area of fertile land eminently suited for development and for which there is ample water available for irrigation," and that "the grant of the land has led to speculation on a considerable scale."

*Huleh Area*

For twenty years (from 1914 to 1934) the Huleh Concession—some 57,000 dunams of partly swamp-infested but potentially highly fertile land in northeastern Palestine—was in Arab hands. The Arab concessionaires were to drain and develop the land so as to make additional tracts available for cultivation, under very attractive terms offered by the Government (first Turkish, then British). However, this was never done, and in 1934 the concession was sold to a Jewish concern, the Palestine Land Development Company, at a huge profit. The Government added several onerous conditions concerning the amount of land (from the drained and newly developed tracts) that had to be handed over—without reimbursement for drainage and irrigation costs —to Arab tenant-farmers in the area.

All told, hundreds of millions of dollars were paid by Jewish buyers to Arab landowners. Official records show that in 1933 £854,796 was paid by Jewish individuals and organizations for Arab land, mostly large estates; in 1934 the figure was £1,647,836 and in 1935, £1,699,488. Thus, in the course of only three years £4,202,180 (more than 20 million dollars at the prevailing rate of exchange) was paid out to Arab landowners (Palestine Royal Commission Report, 1937).

To understand the magnitude of the prices paid for these lands, we need only look at some comparative figures. In 1944, Jews paid between $1,000 and $1,100 per acre in Palestine, mostly for arid or semi-arid land; in the same year rich black soil in the state of Iowa was selling for about $110 per acre (U.S. Department of Agriculture).

*Effects on Arab Population*

In those instances where as a result of such transactions Arab tenant-farmers were displaced (on one year's notice), compensation in cash or other land was paid, as required by the 1922 Protection of Cultivators Ordinance; the Jewish land-buying associations often paid more than the law required (Pollack and Boehm, *The Keren Kayemeth*

*Le-Israel*). Of 688 such tenants between 1920 and 1930, 526 remained in agricultural occupations, some 400 of them finding other land (Palestine Royal Commission Report, 1937, Chapter 9, para. 61).

Investigations initiated in 1931 by Mr. Lewis French disposed of the charge that a large class of landless or dispossessed Arab farmers was created as a result of Jewish land purchases. According to the British Government report (Memoranda prepared by the Government of Palestine, London 1937, Colonia No. 133, p. 37), the total number of applications for registration as landless Arabs was 3,271. Of these, 2,607 were rejected on the ground that they did not come within the category of landless Arabs. Valid claims were recognized in the case of 664 heads of families, of whom 347 accepted the offer of resettlement by the Government. The remainder refused either because they had found satisfactory employment elsewhere or because they were not accustomed to irrigated cultivation or the climate of the new areas (Peel Report, Chapter 9, para. 60).

Purchases of land by Jews in the hill country had always been very small and, according to the investigations by Mr. French, of 71 applications by Arabs claiming to be landless, 68 were turned down.

### *Arab Population Changes Due to Jewish Settlement*

Another Arab claim disproved by the facts is that Zionist "colonialism" led to the disruption and ruin of the Arab Palestinian society and economy.

Statistics published in the Palestine Royal Commission Report (p. 279) indicate a remarkable phenomenon: Palestine, traditionally a country of Arab emigration, became after World War I a country of Arab immigration. In addition to recorded figures for 1920–36, the Report devotes a special section to illegal Arab immigration. While there are no precise totals on the extent of Arab immigration between the two World Wars, estimates vary between 60,000 and 100,000. The principal cause of the change of direction was Jewish development, which created new and attractive work opportunities and, in general, a standard of living previously unknown in the Middle East.

Another major factor in the rapid growth of the Arab population was, of course, the rate of natural increase, among the highest in the world. This was accentuated by the steady reduction of the previously high infant mortality rate as a result of the improved health and sanitary conditions introduced by the Jews.

Altogether, the non-Jewish element in Palestine's population (not including Bedouin) expanded between 1922 and 1929 alone by more than 75 percent. The Royal Commission Report makes these interesting observations:

> The shortage of land is, we consider, due less to the amount of land acquired by Jews than to the increase in the Arab population. (p. 242) We are also of the opinion that up till now the Arab cultivator has benefited, on the whole, both from the work of the British administration and from the presence of Jews in the country. Wages have gone up; the standard of living has improved; work on roads and buildings has been plentiful. In the Maritime Plains some Arabs have adopted improved methods of cultivation. (p. 241)

Jewish development served as an incentive not only to Arab entry into Palestine from Lebanon, Egypt, Syria and other neighboring countries, but also to Arab population movements within the country—to cities and areas where there was a large Jewish concentration. Some idea of this phenomenon may be gained from the following official figures:

*Changes in towns:* The Arab population in predominantly Arab towns rose only slightly (if at all) between the two World Wars: in Hebron—from 16,650 in 1922 to 22,800 in 1943; Nablus—from 15,931 to 23,300; Jenin—from 2,737 to 3,900; Bethlehem—from 6,658 to 8,800. Gaza's population actually decreased from 17,426 in 1922 to 17,045 in 1931.

On the other hand, in the three major Jewish cities the Arab population shot up during this period, far beyond the rate of natural increase: Jerusalem—from 28,571 in 1922 to 56,400 (97 percent); Jaffa —from 27,437 to 62,600 (134 percent); Haifa—from 18,404 to 58,200 (216 percent).

*Changes in rural areas:* The population of the predominantly Arab Beersheba district dropped between 1922 and 1939 from 71,000 to 49,000 (the rate of natural increase should have resulted in a rise to 89,000). In the Bethlehem district the figure increased from 24,613 to about 26,000 (after falling to 23,725 in 1929). In the Hebron area it went up from 51,345 to 59,000 (the natural increase rate dictated a rise to 72,000).

In contrast to these declines or comparatively slight increases in exclusively Arab-inhabited areas, in the Nazareth, Beit Shean, Tiberias and Acre districts—where large-scale Jewish settlement and rural development was underway—the figure rose from 89,600 in 1922 to some 151,000 in 1938 (by about 4.5 percent per annum, compared with a natural increase rate of 2.5–3 percent).

In the largely Jewish Haifa area the number of Arab peasants increased by 8 percent a year during the same period. In the Jaffa and Ramla districts (heavily Jewish populated), the Arab rural population grew from 42,300 to some 126,000—an annual increase of 12 percent, or more than four times as much as can be attributed to natural increase (L. Shimony, *The Arabs of Palestine,* Tel-Aviv, 1947, pp. 422-23).

One reason for the Arab gravitation toward Jewish-inhabited areas, and from neighboring countries to Palestine, was the incomparably higher wage scales paid there, as may be seen from the following table.

DAILY WAGE SCALES, 1943
(in mils)

| | *Unskilled labor* | *Skilled labor* |
|---|---|---|
| Palestine | 220–250 | 350–600 |
| Egypt | 30–50 | 70–200 |
| Syria | 80–100 | 150–300 |
| Iraq | 50 | 70–200 |

Source: A. Khoushy, *Brit Poali Eretz-Israel,* 1943, p. 25.

The capital received by Arab landowners for their surplus holdings was used for improved and intensive cultivation or invested in other enterprises. Turning again to the Report of the Palestine Royal Commission (p. 93), we find the following conclusions: "The large import of Jewish capital into Palestine has had a general fructifying effect on the economic life of the whole country. . . . The expansion of Arab industry and citriculture has been largely financed by the capital thus obtained. . . . Jewish example has done much to improve Arab cultivation. . . . The increase in Arab population is most marked in areas affected by Jewish development."

During World War II, the Arab population influx mounted apace, as is attested by the *UNRWA Review,* Information Paper No. 6 (September 1962):

> A considerable movement of people is known to have occurred, particularly during the Second World War, years when new opportunities of employment opened up in the towns and on military works in Palestine. These wartime prospects and, generally, the higher rate of industrialization in Palestine attracted many new immigrants from the neighboring countries, and many of them entered Palestine without their presence being officially recorded.

*Land Ownership in 1948*

The claim is often made that in 1948 a Jewish minority owning only 5 percent of the land of Palestine made itself master of the Arab majority, which owned 95 percent of the land.

In May 1948 the State of Israel was established in only part of the area allotted by the original League of Nations Mandate. 8.6 percent of the land was owned by Jews and 3.3 percent by Israeli Arabs, while 16.9 percent had been abandoned by Arab owners who imprudently heeded the call from neighboring countries to "get out of the way" while the invading Arab armies make short shrift of Israel. The rest of the land—over 70 percent—had been vested in the Mandatory Power, and accordingly reverted to the State of Israel as its legal heir. (Government of Palestine, *Survey of Palestine, 1946,* British Government Printer, p. 257.)

The greater part of this 70 percent consisted of the Negev, some 3,144,250 acres all told, or close to 50 percent of the 6,580,000 acres in all of Mandatory Palestine. Known as Crown or State Lands, this was mostly uninhabited arid or semi-arid territory, inherited originally by the Mandatory Government from Turkey. In 1948 it passed to the Government of Israel.

These lands had not been owned by Arab farmers—neither under the British Mandate nor under the preceding regime. Thus it is obvious that the contention that 95 percent of the land—whether of Mandatory Palestine or of the State of Israel—had belonged to Arabs has absolutely no foundation in fact.

* * *

There is perhaps no better way of concluding and summing up this study than to quote from an article entitled *Is Israel a Thorn or a Flower in the Near East?* by Abdul Razak Kader, the Algerian political writer, now living in exile in Paris (*Jerusalem Post,* Aug. 1, 1969):

"The Nationalists of the states neighboring on Israel, whether they are in the government or in business, whether Palestinian, Syrian or Lebanese, or town dwellers of tribal origin, all know that at the beginning of the century and during the British Mandate the marshy plains and stony hills were sold to the Zionists by their fathers or uncles for gold, the very gold which is often the origin of their own political or commercial careers. The nomadic or semi-nomadic peasants who inhabited the frontier regions know full well what the green plains, the afforested hills and the flowering fields of today's Israel were like before.

"The Palestinians who are today refugees in the neighbouring countries and who were adults at the time of their flight know all this, and no anti-Zionist propaganda—pan-Arab or pan-Moslem—can make them forget that their present nationalist exploiters are the worthy sons of their feudal exploiters of yesterday and that the thorns of their life are of Arab, not Jewish, origin."

## Appendix II

# THE PALESTINIAN NATIONAL COVENANT*

*Commentary and Analysis by Yoshua Harkabi*

---

* Appeared in (1970), 5 *N. Y. U. Journal of International Law and Politics* 228.

The Palestinian National Covenant is perhaps the most important document of this stage of the Israel-Arab conflict, especially with regard to the Arab side. It represents a summation of the official position of the Palestinian organizations in the conflict.

The previous version of the Covenant was adopted by the First Palestinian Congress, which convened in Jerusalem in May, 1964 at the time of the establishment of the Palestine Liberation Organization. In the official English translation of the previous version it was called "Covenant" and not "Charter," in order to emphasize its national sanctity, and the introductory words to the Covenant conclude with an oath to implement it. The Congress stipulated that a Palestinian National Council, the highest institution of the Palestinian organizations, would meet periodically, and that a two-thirds majority of the Council members would be required to amend the Covenant. As a result of the changes which came about in the Palestine Liberation Organization after the Six-Day War the Palestinian National Council convened in Cairo for its fourth session on July 10-17, 1968 and amended the Covenant. It should be noted that representatives of almost all the Palestinian organizations existing in Arab countries participated in this session, including all the Fedayeen organizations. Fatah and the fedayeen organizations under its influence had thirty-seven representatives in the National Council of one hundred members and the Popular Front had ten. Fatah's style is recognizable in the new Covenant. This amended version was certainly not formulated casually; it represents a position that was seriously considered and weighed. The amended version is here presented. In order to highlight the changes we shall compare this version with its predecessor.

The main principles which were set down in the Covenant are:

In the Palestinian State only Jews who lived in Palestine before 1917 will be recognized as citizens (Article 6).

Only the Palestinian Arabs possess the right of self-determination, and the entire country belongs to them (Articles 3 and 21).

Any solution that does not involve total liberation of the country is rejected. This aim cannot be achieved politically; it can only be accomplished militarily (Articles 9 and 21).

Warfare against Israel is legal, whereas Israel's self-defense is illegal (Article 18).

For the sake of completeness the Covenant is presented here in its entirety.

## THE PALESTINIAN NATIONAL COVENANT

(The body of the document is translated from the Arabic original. Articles of the 1964 Covenant repeated here are rendered on the basis of the official English translation of that Covenant but with alterations of style and terminology. The same procedure is followed in translating quotations from the earlier Covenant cited in the commentary.)

THIS COVENANT WILL BE CALLED "THE PALESTINIAN NATIONAL COVENANT (*AL-MÎ THÂQ AL-WATANÎ AL-FÎLASTÎNÎ*)."

In the previous version of the Covenant of May, 1964 the adjective "national" was rendered by *qawmî,* the usual meaning of which in modern Arabic is pan-Arab and ethnic nationalism, whereas here they use the adjective *watanî,* which signifies nationalism in its narrow, territorialistic sense as patriotism toward a specific country. This change intends to stress Palestinian patriotism.

## ARTICLES OF THE COVENANT

ARTICLE 1) PALESTINE IS THE HOMELAND OF THE PALESTINIAN ARAB PEOPLE AND AN INTEGRAL PART OF THE GREAT ARAB HOMELAND, AND THE PEOPLE OF PALESTINE IS A PART OF THE ARAB NATION.

In most Arab constitutions it is simply stipulated that the people of that country constitutes an integral part of the Arab nation. Here, because of the special problem of territory, it is also stressed that the land is an integral part of the general Arab homeland. The previous version in the Covenant of 1964 was more vague: "Palestine is an Arab homeland bound by strong Arab national ties to the rest of the Arab countries which together form the Great Arab Homeland." The combination "the Palestinian Arab people" recurs often in the Covenant and is also intended to stress the special status of the Palestinians, though as Arabs.

ARTICLE 2) PALESTINE WITH ITS BOUNDARIES THAT EXISTED AT THE TIME OF THE BRITISH MANDATE IS AN INTEGRAL REGIONAL UNIT.

The same formulation as in the previous version. It is implied that Palestine should not be divided into a Jewish and an Arab state. Although it is an accepted tenet of Arab nationalism that existing boundaries should be abolished, since they were artificially delineated by the imperialist powers, here they are sanctified. The expression "that existed at the time of the British Mandate" is vague. The article is subject to two interpretations: 1) The Palestinian State includes also Jordan and thus supersedes it; 2) The West Bank is detached from Jordan.

ARTICLE 3) THE PALESTINIAN ARAB PEOPLE POSSESSES THE LEGAL RIGHT TO ITS HOMELAND, AND WHEN THE LIBERATION OF ITS HOMELAND IS COMPLETED IT WILL EXERCISE SELF-DETERMINATION SOLELY ACCORDING TO ITS OWN WILL AND CHOICE.

The decision concerning the problem of the internal regime is deferred until after the liberation. The crux of this article is to postpone the decision concerning the relation to the Kingdom of Jordan and Hashemite rule. There is also the emphasis here that only the Palestinian Arabs possess a national legal right, excluding of course the Jews, to whom a special article is devoted below.

ARTICLE 4) THE PALESTINIAN PERSONALITY IS AN INNATE, PERSISTENT CHARACTERISTIC THAT DOES NOT DISAPPEAR, AND IT IS TRANSFERRED FROM FATHERS TO SONS. THE ZIONIST OCCUPATION, AND THE DISPERSAL OF THE PALESTINIAN ARAB PEOPLE AS A RESULT OF THE DISASTERS WHICH CAME OVER IT, DO NOT DEPRIVE IT OF ITS PALESTINIAN PERSONALITY AND AFFILIATION AND DO NOT NULLIFY THEM.

The Palestinian, therefore, cannot cease being a Palestinian. Palestinianism is not citizenship but an eternal characteristic that comes from birth. The Jew is a Jew through the maternal line, and the Palestinian a Palestinian through the paternal line. The Palestinians, consequently, cannot be assimilated. This article implies that Palestinian citizenship follows from the Palestinian characteristics. This is the Palestinian counterpart to the Law of Return.

ARTICLE 5) THE PALESTINIANS ARE THE ARAB CITIZENS WHO WERE LIVING PERMANENTLY IN PALESTINE UNTIL 1947, WHETHER THEY WERE EXPELLED FROM THERE OR REMAINED. WHOEVER IS BORN TO A PALESTINIAN ARAB FATHER AFTER THIS DATE, WITHIN PALESTINE OR OUTSIDE IT, IS A PALESTINIAN.

A reinforcement of the previous article. This definition refers solely to the Arabs. With reference to the Jews the matter is different. This is because being Palestinian is basically equivalent to being Arab.

ARTICLE 6) JEWS WHO WERE LIVING PERMANENTLY IN PALESTINE UNTIL THE BEGINNING OF THE ZIONIST INVASION WILL BE CONSIDERED PALESTINIANS.

In the section on resolutions of the Congress, in the chapter entitled "The International Palestinian Struggle" (p. 51), it is stated: "Likewise, the National Council affirms that the aggression against the Arab nation and its land began with the Zionist invasion of Palestine in 1917. Therefore, the meaning of "removal of the traces of the aggression" must be removal of the traces of the aggression which came into effect from the beginning of the Zionist invasion and not from the war of June, 1967. . . ."

"The beginning of the Zionist invasion" is therefore at the time of the Balfour Declaration. This conception is current in Arab political literature. In the 1964 .version the corresponding article was: "Jews of Palestinian origin will be considered Palestinians if they are willing to endeavor to live in loyalty and peace in Palestine." The expression "of Palestinian origin" is vague, for the article does not specify which Jews are to be considered of Palestinian origin. Since in the previous article (5 in the new version, 6 in the old) the date which determines being Palestinian is set at 1947, the implication could be that this applies also to the Jews. Since the aim is the return of the Arab Palestinians, it is necessary to make room for them. However, in the meantime, Jews have taken up residence in Arab dwelling-places, especially those Jews who immigrated after 1947; hence also from a practical aspect it is necessary to remove these Jews in particular.

The Jews who will not be recognized as Palestinians are therefore aliens who have no right of residence and must leave.

The National Covenant is a public document intended for general distribution. The Executive Committee of the Palestine Liberation Organization specified in its introduction to the official report of the proceedings of the Congress as follows: "In view of the importance of the resolutions of the Palestinian National Council in its session convened in Cairo from July 10 to 17, 1968, we publish them in this booklet so that the Palestinians in every place may read them and find in them a policy and a program. . . ." (pp. 17-18).

One might expect that those hundred members of the National Council would have recoiled from adopting such an extreme position which could serve as a weapon against the Palestinians. The fact that they did not is itself of great significance and testifies to the severity of the Palestinian Arab position.

A year and a half has elapsed since the Covenant was amended, sufficient time to raise criticism against this manifestation of extremism. However, until now no Arab body, including the Popular Front for the Liberation of Palestine, which is usually critical of the Palestine Liberation Organization and Fatah, has dissociated itself from the position presented in this article. To the best of my knowledge, no article has been published in an Arab newspaper that raises criticism against it. This silence is also highly significant.

The amended version of this article points to a radicalization of the Palestinian Arab position. It contains decisive evidence as to the nature of the slogan Arab leaders brandish concerning a "pluralistic, democratic state." Pluralism that is expressed in the elimination of two million four hundred thousand Israeli Jews is nothing but throwing dust in the eyes.

Arab spokesmen add that the aim is for the Palestinian state to be secular, as opposed to Israel, which they condemn as an anachronistic state founded upon a religious principle. It should be noted, however, that in all the constitutions of the Arab states (except Lebanon) Islam is explicitly established as the state religion. The Syrian constitution of 1964 stipulates that the president of the state must be a Muslim. In most of the constitutions it is also emphasized that the *Sharî'a* (Islamic Law) is the source of the laws of the state. Fatah appealed to a congress held in al-Azhar University in September, 1968 to consider contributions to the fedayeen *Zakât* (a religious alms tax) and warfare against Israel, *Jihâd*. Thus they wage a religious war in order to establish a secular state. The crown of democracy, with which Palestinian spokesmen adorn the Palestinian state, also arouses scepticism in view of the Arabs' failure to set up democratic regimes.

Even if the Palestinians, realizing how this article damages their cause, amend it, such an amendment would be tactical and reactive, a response to foreign criticism, while the 1968 version reflects the more spontaneous mood.

ARTICLE 7) THE PALESTINIAN AFFILIATION AND THE MATERIAL, SPIRITUAL AND HISTORICAL TIE WITH PALESTINE ARE PERMANENT REALITIES. THE UPBRINGING OF THE PALESTINIAN INDIVIDUAL IN AN ARAB AND REVOLUTIONARY FASHION, THE UNDERTAKING OF ALL MEANS OF FORGING CONSCIOUSNESS AND TRAINING THE PALESTINIAN, IN ORDER TO ACQUAINT HIM PROFOUNDLY WITH HIS HOMELAND, SPIRITUALLY AND MATERIALLY, AND PREPARING HIM FOR THE CONFLICT AND THE ARMED STRUGGLE, AS WELL AS FOR THE SACRIFICE OF HIS PROPERTY AND HIS LIFE TO RESTORE HIS HOMELAND, UNTIL THE LIBERATION—ALL THIS IS A NATIONAL DUTY.

The second part, the preparation for the struggle, is new and was formulated under the influence of the special place that is now given to fedayeenism.

ARTICLE 8) THE PHASE IN WHICH THE PEOPLE OF PALESTINE IS LIVING IS THAT OF THE NATIONAL (*WATANĪ*) STRUGGLE FOR THE LIBERATION OF PALESTINE. THEREFORE, THE CONTRADICTIONS AMONG THE PALESTINIAN NATIONAL FORCES ARE OF A SECONDARY ORDER WHICH MUST BE SUSPENDED IN THE INTEREST OF THE FUNDAMENTAL CONTRADICTION BETWEEN ZIONISM AND COLONIALISM ON THE ONE SIDE AND THE PALESTINIAN ARAB PEOPLE ON THE OTHER. ON THIS BASIS, THE PALESTINIAN MASSES, WHETHER IN THE HOMELAND OR IN PLACES OF EXILE (*MAHĀJIR*), ORGANIZATIONS AND INDIVIDUALS, COMPRISE ONE NATIONAL FRONT WHICH ACTS TO RESTORE PALESTINE AND LIBERATE IT THROUGH ARMED STRUGGLE.

It is necessary to postpone internal disputes and concentrate on warfare against Israel. The style of "secondary contradictions" and "fundamental contradictions" is influenced by the language of Fatah and the younger circles. In the previous corresponding article it is stated: "Doctrines, whether political, social or economic, shall not divert the people of Palestine from their primary duty of liberating their homeland. . . ."

ARTICLE 9) ARMED STRUGGLE IS THE ONLY WAY TO LIBERATE PALESTINE AND IS THEREFORE A STRATEGY AND NOT TACTICS. THE PALESTINIAN ARAB PEOPLE AFFIRMS ITS ABSOLUTE RESOLUTION AND ABIDING DETERMINATION TO PURSUE THE ARMED STRUGGLE AND TO MARCH FORWARD TOWARD THE ARMED POPULAR REVOLUTION, TO LIBERATE ITS HOMELAND AND RETURN TO IT, [TO MAINTAIN] ITS RIGHT TO A NATURAL LIFE IN IT, AND TO EXERCISE ITS RIGHT OF SELF-DETERMINATION IN IT AND SOVEREIGNTY OVER IT.

The expression "a strategy and not tactics" is from the lexicon of Fatah expressions (see Y. Harkabi, *Fedayeen Action and Arab Strategy* [Adelphi Papers, No. 53, The Institute for Strategic Studies, London, 1968], p. 8). They use it with reference to fedayeen activities: they are not a support weapon but the essence of the war. "The armed struggle" is a broader concept, but here too stress is placed on action of the fedayeen variety. "The armed popular revolution" signifies the participation of the entire people in the war against Israel. It is depicted as a stage that will be reached by means of broadening the activity of the fedayeen. They are merely the vanguard whose role is to produce a "detonation" of the revolution until it embraces all levels of the people.

The radicalism in the aim of annihilation of the State of Israel and the "liberation" of all its territory eliminates the possibility of a political solution, which is by nature a compromise settlement. Such is the reasoning in this article and in Article 21. There remains only the way of violence.

ARTICLE 10) FEDAYEEN ACTION FORMS THE NUCLEUS OF THE POPULAR PALESTINIAN WAR OF LIBERATION. THIS DEMANDS ITS PROMOTION, EXTENSION AND PROTECTION, AND THE MOBILIZATION OF ALL THE MASS AND SCIENTIFIC CAPACITIES OF THE PALESTINIANS, THEIR ORGANIZATION AND INVOLVEMENT IN THE ARMED PALESTINIAN REVOLUTION, AND COHESION IN THE NATIONAL (*WATANĪ*) STRUGGLE AMONG THE VARIOUS GROUPS OF THE PEOPLE OF PALESTINE, AND BETWEEN THEM AND THE ARAB MASSES, TO GUARANTEE THE CONTINUATION OF THE REVOLUTION, ITS ADVANCEMENT AND VICTORY.

This article is new. It describes the "alchemy" of fedayeenism, how its activity broadens and eventually sweeps the entire people. The masses in Arab countries are described in the language of Fatah as constituting "the supportive Arab front," the role of which is not only to offer aid but to assure that the Arab states will not deviate, on account of local interests and pressures, from their obligation to support the Palestinian revolution.

ARTICLE 11) THE PALESTINIANS WILL HAVE THREE MOTTOES: NATIONAL (*WATANIYYA*) UNITY, NATIONAL (*QAWMIYYA*) MOBILIZATION AND LIBERATION.

Here there is no change. These mottoes are inscribed above the publications of the Palestine Liberation Organization.

ARTICLE 12) THE PALESTINIAN ARAB PEOPLE BELIEVES IN ARAB UNITY. IN ORDER TO FULFILL ITS ROLE IN REALIZING THIS, IT MUST PRESERVE, IN THIS PHASE OF ITS NATIONAL (*WATANI*) STRUGGLE, ITS PALESTINIAN PERSONALITY AND THE CONSTITUENTS THEREOF, INCREASE CONSCIOUSNESS OF ITS EXISTENCE AND RESIST ANY PLAN THAT TENDS TO DISINTEGRATE OR WEAKEN IT.

The idea of Arab unity requires giving priority to the pan-Arab character over the local character. From the aspect of a consistent doctrine of unity, stressing local character or distinctiveness is divisive because it strengthens difference, whereas unity rests on what is common and uniform. The issue of the relation between local distinctiveness and pan-Arab unity has much preoccupied the ideologues of Arab nationalism. The conservative circles tend to stress the need for preserving local character even after unity has been achieved. By this means Arab unity will be enriched through variegation. The revolutionary circles, on the other hand, stress unity and homogeneity. This is based either on a practical consideration, that internal consolidation will be reinforced in proportion to the reduction of distinctive factors, or on the view that the local character is part of the heritage they wish to change. The controversy between distinctiveness and unity is also reflected in the conception of the structure of unity. Those who seek to preserve distinctiveness deem it necessary to conserve the existing political frameworks in a loosely confederated unified structure. Those who stress unity tend to try and obliterate the existing political frameworks, along with their boundaries, which were merely the adjunct of a colonial system, with the object of achieving a more consolidated political structure. This controversy may be represented as an antinomy in which Arab nationalism is caught: Unity which tries to suppress the distinctive character of its parts will arouse local opposition; unity which conserves the local distinctive character may abet divisive tendencies.

This article intends to answer the charge that stressing Palestinian distinctiveness is an objective that conflicts with Arab unity (in the language of Arab nationalism, the sin of *Shu'ûbiyya* or *Iqlîmiyya*). This charge was heard, for example, from within circles of the Qawmiyyûn al-'Arab movement, who were dedicated to the idea of Arab unity. Previous to the Six-Day War this charge also had a practical aspect, namely, the assessment that excessive stress on the Palestinianism of the struggle against Israel diminished the role of the Arab states as direct participants in this confrontation. The response to this charge is, therefore, that preservation of Palestinian distinctiveness is merely a temporary necessity, to be transcended in favor of Arab unity. There is, however, a contradiction between this contention and the previous assertion of the eternity of the Palestinian personality.

ARTICLE 13) ARAB UNITY AND THE LIBERATION OF PALESTINE ARE TWO COMPLEMENTARY AIMS. EACH ONE PAVES THE WAY FOR REALIZATION OF THE OTHER. ARAB UNITY LEADS TO THE LIBERATION OF PALESTINE, AND THE LIBERATION OF PALESTINE LEADS TO ARAB UNITY. WORKING FOR BOTH GOES HAND IN HAND.

This again is an antinomy. Victory over Israel requires concentration of all Arab forces upon the struggle, a concentration made possible only by the establishment of a supra-state authority to control all these forces, that is, a common government. Nasser repeatedly warned that unity is a precondition for initiating war against Israel. But attaining unity is a long-range affair. Consequently, war against Israel is deferred until a remote time, because undertaking a war without unity would only lead to defeat. On the other hand, unity can be attained only by the detonation of a spectacular event, like victory over Israel. The ideologues of Fatah were much preoccupied with this issue (see *Fedayeen Action and Arab Strategy,* p. 9). Their response is contained in their slogan: "The liberation of Palestine is the road to unity, and this is the right substitute for the slogan, 'unity is the road to the liberation of Palestine.' " Actually, this article offers a verbal solution, circumventing the problem of priority by characterizing both events as contemporary, just as in the previous version of the Covenant.

ARTICLE 14) THE DESTINY OF THE ARAB NATION, INDEED THE VERY ARAB EXISTENCE, DEPENDS UPON THE DESTINY OF THE PALESTINE ISSUE. THE ENDEAVOR AND EFFORT OF THE ARAB NATION TO LIBERATE PALESTINE FOLLOWS FROM THIS CONNECTION. THE PEOPLE OF PALESTINE ASSUMES ITS VANGUARD ROLE IN REALIZING THIS SACRED NATIONAL (*QAWMĪ*) AIM.

This is a common notion in the Arab position. It is often stated in Arab political literature that the Palestine issue is *fateful* for the very Arab existence. It is maintained that the existence of Israel prevents the Arabs from achieving their national goal. Furthermore, the existence of Israel necessarily leads to its expansion and the liquidation of the Arabness of additional Arab lands. The Palestinians have an interest in stressing the fatefulness of the struggle against Israel and its centrality for the whole Arab world. They thus spur on the others to take an active role in the struggle against Israel. It may be that there is also hidden here the intention to lend symmetry to the conflict. Thus, both sides threaten each other with extinction, and the Arabs are not alone in this. A formula for division of labor is also presented here. The Palestinians will be the vanguard marching before the Arab camp.

ARTICLE 15) THE LIBERATION OF PALESTINE, FROM AN ARAB VIEWPOINT, IS A NATIONAL (*QAWMĪ*) DUTY TO REPULSE THE ZIONIST, IMPERIALIST INVASION FROM THE GREAT ARAB HOMELAND AND TO PURGE THE ZIONIST PRESENCE FROM PALESTINE. ITS FULL RESPONSIBILITIES FALL UPON THE ARAB NATION, PEOPLES AND GOVERNMENTS, WITH THE PALESTINIAN ARAB PEOPLE AT THEIR HEAD.

The goal is, therefore, twofold: defense of the rest of the Arab countries and removal of Zionism from Palestine.

FOR THIS PURPOSE, THE ARAB NATION MUST MOBILIZE ALL ITS MILITARY, HUMAN, MATERIAL AND SPIRITUAL CAPACITIES TO PARTICIPATE ACTIVELY WITH THE PEOPLE OF PALESTINE IN THE LIBERATION OF PALESTINE. THEY MUST, ESPECIALLY IN THE PRESENT STAGE OF

ARMED PALESTINIAN REVOLUTION, GRANT AND OFFER THE PEOPLE OF PALESTINE ALL POSSIBLE HELP AND EVERY MATERIAL AND HUMAN SUPPORT, AND AFFORD IT EVERY SURE MEANS AND OPPORTUNITY ENABLING IT TO CONTINUE TO ASSUME ITS VANGUARD ROLE IN PURSUING ITS ARMED REVOLUTION UNTIL THE LIBERATION OF ITS HOMELAND.

There is the implied concern lest, without the support of the Arab states, the drive of "the Palestinian revolution" will dissipate. The distinction of this version as compared with its predecessor, is mainly in the accentuation of "the active participation" of the Arab states and the issue of "the armed Palestinian revolution," which is certainly to be attributed to Fatah's ideological influence upon the Palestine Liberation Organization.

ARTICLE 16) THE LIBERATION OF PALESTINE, FROM A SPIRITUAL VIEWPOINT, WILL PREPARE AN ATMOSPHERE OF TRANQUILITY AND PEACE FOR THE HOLY LAND, IN THE SHADE OF WHICH ALL THE HOLY PLACES WILL BE SAFEGUARDED, AND FREEDOM OF WORSHIP AND VISITATION TO ALL WILL BE GUARANTEED, WITHOUT DISTINCTION OR DISCRIMINATION OF RACE, COLOR, LANGUAGE OR RELIGION. FOR THIS REASON, THE PEOPLE OF PALESTINE LOOKS TO THE SUPPORT OF ALL THE SPIRITUAL FORCES IN THE WORLD.

ARTICLE 17) THE LIBERATION OF PALESTINE, FROM A HUMAN VIEWPOINT, WILL RESTORE TO THE PALESTINIAN MAN HIS DIGNITY, GLORY AND FREEDOM. FOR THIS, THE PALESTINIAN ARAB PEOPLE LOOKS TO THE SUPPORT OF THOSE IN THE WORLD WHO BELIEVE IN THE DIGNITY AND FREEDOM OF MAN.

The very existence of Israel and the lack of a Palestinian homeland create alienation in the Palestinian, for these deprive him of his dignity and bring him to a state of subservience. As long as Israel exists the Palestinian's personality is flawed. This is an addition in the spirit of Fatah which was not in the previous version, and it is probably influenced by recent revolutionary literature, such as the teaching of Franz Fanon.

ARTICLE 18) THE LIBERATION OF PALESTINE, FROM AN INTERNATIONAL VIEWPOINT, IS A DEFENSIVE ACT NECESSITATED BY THE REQUIREMENTS OF SELF-DEFENSE. FOR THIS REASON, THE PEOPLE OF PALESTINE, DESIRING TO BEFRIEND ALL PEOPLES, LOOKS TO THE SUPPORT OF THE STATES WHICH LOVE FREEDOM, JUSTICE AND PEACE IN

RESTORING THE LEGAL SITUATION TO PALESTINE, ESTABLISHING SECURITY AND PEACE IN ITS TERRITORY, AND ENABLING ITS PEOPLE TO EXERCISE NATIONAL (*WATANIYYA*) SOVEREIGNTY AND NATIONAL (*QAWMIYYA*) FREEDOM.

As in the previous version, the existence of Israel is illegal; therefore war against it is legal. In Palestinian literature there is a frequent claim that the fedayeen assaults against Israel are legal, while the self-defense and reactions of Israel are illegal, for their aim is to perpetuate the state which embodies aggression in its very establishment and existence. To the foreign observer this distinction between the legality of attacking Israel and the illegality of the response may appear as sham innocence that is indeed even ludicrous. Nevertheless, it may be assumed that there are Arabs for whom this is not only a matter of formal argument but a belief.

Ibrahim al-'Abid, in an article entitled "The Reasons for the Latest Israeli Aggression" (The Six-Day War), writes: "Fedayeen action is a right of the people of Palestine because the right of national liberation is an extension of the right of peoples to self-defense, and it is the right which the United Nations Charter affirmed as an original natural right." (Anis Sayegh, ed., *Filastíniyyâat,* PLO Center for Research, Beirut, 1968, p. 107).

ARTICLE 19) THE PARTITIONING OF PALESTINE IN 1947 AND THE ESTABLISHMENT OF ISRAEL IS FUNDAMENTALLY NULL AND VOID, WHATEVER TIME HAS ELAPSED, BECAUSE IT WAS CONTRARY TO THE WISH OF THE PEOPLE OF PALESTINE AND ITS NATURAL RIGHT TO ITS HOMELAND, AND CONTRADICTS THE PRINCIPLES EMBODIED IN THE CHARTER OF THE UNITED NATIONS, THE FIRST OF WHICH IS THE RIGHT OF SELF-DETERMINATION.

It is often found in Arab literature that the Mandate and the Partition Resolution, though accepted by the League of Nations and the United Nations Organization, have no legal force. They represent an aberration and not a norm of international law. The reason for this is that they contradicted the fundamental principle of the right of self-determination. This article is copied from the previous version.

ARTICLE 20) THE BALFOUR DECLARATION, THE MANDATE DOCUMENT, AND WHAT HAS BEEN BASED UPON THEM ARE CONSIDERED NULL AND VOID. THE CLAIM OF A HISTORICAL OR SPIRITUAL TIE BETWEEN JEWS AND PALESTINE DOES NOT TALLY WITH HISTORICAL REALITIES NOR WITH THE CONSTITUENTS OF STATEHOOD IN THEIR TRUE SENSE. JUDAISM, IN ITS CHARACTER AS A RELIGION OF

REVELATION, IS NOT A NATIONALITY WITH AN INDEPENDENT EXISTENCE. LIKEWISE, THE JEWS ARE NOT ONE PEOPLE WITH AN INDEPENDENT PERSONALITY. THEY ARE RATHER CITIZENS OF THE STATES TO WHICH THEY BELONG.

Again an identical formulation. This article incorporates the principal claims concerning historical right: The Jews lived in Palestine for only a brief time; their sovereignty over it was not exclusive; the Arabs did not conquer it from them and need not restore it to them; and the Arabs remained in the country longer than the Jews. Moreover, a state embodies a national, not a religious, principle. The Jews, as having merely religious distinctiveness, do not need a state at all, and a Jewish state that makes of Judaism a nationalism is a historical and political aberration. Therefore, Zionism, as a manifestation of Jewish nationalism, distorts Judaism.

Since the State of Israel is not based on a true nationalism, it is very often described in Arabic as "an artificial entity." This is also brought as proof that Israel can be destroyed. This conception is also at the basis of fedayeen theory: since the Jews have no real nationalism, terror will cause their disintegration to the point that they will consent to relinquish Jewish statehood.

The conception that the Jews do not constitute a national entity is a vital principle for the Arab position. For if the Israelis are a nation, then they have the right of self-determination, and the claim that only the Palestinian Arabs have the right of self-determination, and that only they must decide the national character of the country, is not valid. Moreover, the Arab claim for exclusive national self-determination appears in all its starkness as chauvinism that demands everything for itself while denying any right to the other.

ARTICLE 21) THE PALESTINIAN ARAB PEOPLE, IN EXPRESSING ITSELF THROUGH THE ARMED PALESTINIAN REVOLUTION, REJECTS EVERY SOLUTION THAT IS A SUBSTITUTE FOR A COMPLETE LIBERATION OF PALESTINE, AND REJECTS ALL PLANS THAT AIM AT THE SETTLEMENT OF THE PALESTINE ISSUE OR ITS INTERNATIONALIZATION.

This rejection of any compromise settlement is an addition to the previous version. In the resolutions of the fourth session of the Palestinian National Council a long and detailed section is devoted to the rejection of the Security Council Resolution of November 22, 1967 and any peaceful solution, with insistence upon the intention to undermine any attempt in this direction.

ARTICLE 22) ZIONISM IS A POLITICAL MOVEMENT ORGANICALLY RELATED TO WORLD IMPERIALISM AND HOS-

TILE TO ALL MOVEMENTS OF LIBERATION AND PROGRESS IN THE WORLD. IT IS A RACIST AND FANATICAL MOVEMENT IN ITS FORMATION; AGGRESSIVE, EXPANSIONIST AND COLONIALIST IN ITS AIMS; AND FASCIST AND NAZI IN ITS MEANS. ISRAEL IS THE TOOL OF THE ZIONIST MOVEMENT AND A HUMAN AND GEOGRAPHICAL BASE FOR WORLD IMPERIALISM. IT IS A CONCENTRATION AND JUMPING-OFF POINT FOR IMPERIALISM IN THE HEART OF THE ARAB HOMELAND, TO STRIKE AT THE HOPES OF THE ARAB NATION FOR LIBERATION, UNITY AND PROGRESS.

In this new version there is an accentuation of Israel's relation to world imperialism and intensification of its denunciation. This is in the spirit of the Leftist sentiments that prevail among the up-and-coming Arab generation. The claim that the hostility of Zionism is directed, not only against the Arabs, but against all that is good in the world, is also an addition. Thus, warfare against Israel is elevated from an Arab interest to a universal humanistic mission.

ISRAEL IS A CONSTANT THREAT TO PEACE IN THE MIDDLE EAST AND THE ENTIRE WORLD. SINCE THE LIBERATION OF PALESTINE WILL LIQUIDATE THE ZIONIST AND IMPERIALIST PRESENCE AND BRING ABOUT THE STABILIZATION OF PEACE IN THE MIDDLE EAST, THE PEOPLE OF PALESTINE LOOKS TO THE SUPPORT OF ALL LIBERAL MEN OF THE WORLD AND ALL THE FORCES OF GOOD, PROGRESS AND PEACE; AND IMPLORES ALL OF THEM, REGARDLESS OF THEIR DIFFERENT LEANINGS AND ORIENTATIONS, TO OFFER ALL HELP AND SUPPORT TO THE PEOPLE OF PALESTINE IN ITS JUST AND LEGAL STRUGGLE TO LIBERATE ITS HOMELAND.

ARTICLE 23) THE DEMANDS OF SECURITY AND PEACE AND THE REQUIREMENTS OF TRUTH AND JUSTICE OBLIGE ALL STATES THAT PRESERVE FRIENDLY RELATIONS AMONG PEOPLES AND MAINTAIN THE LOYALTY OF CITIZENS TO THEIR HOMELANDS TO CONSIDER ZIONISM AN ILLEGITIMATE MOVEMENT AND TO PROHIBIT ITS EXISTENCE AND ACTIVITY.

The attachment of Jews to Israel expressed in Zionism creates dual-nationality and political chaos. Arabs apparently do not sense the contradiction in this claim. Despite the prevalence of supranational tendencies among circles in the progressive world, with which the Palestinians claim to have an affinity, a narrow, formal nationalistic approach is stressed here, which maintains that a man cannot cherish a loyal attachment to any factor apart from his own state.

ARTICLE 24) THE PALESTINIAN ARAB PEOPLE BELIEVES IN THE PRINCIPLES OF JUSTICE, FREEDOM, SOVEREIGNTY, SELF-DETERMINATION, HUMAN DIGNITY AND THE RIGHT OF PEOPLES TO EXERCISE THEM.

ARTICLE 25) TO REALIZE THE AIMS OF THIS COVENANT AND ITS PRINCIPLES THE PALESTINE LIBERATION ORGANIZATION WILL UNDERTAKE ITS FULL ROLE IN LIBERATING PALESTINE.

This article (with the omission of the conclusion, "in accordance with the fundamental law of this organization") is identical to the previous version. In this and the next article the Palestine Liberation Organization is presented as the umbrella organization bearing the general responsibility for the struggle of all the Palestinians against Israel.

ARTICLE 26) THE PALESTINE LIBERATION ORGANIZATION, WHICH REPRESENTS THE FORCES OF THE PALESTINIAN REVOLUTION, IS RESPONSIBLE FOR THE MOVEMENT OF THE PALESTINIAN ARAB PEOPLE IN ITS STRUGGLE TO RESTORE ITS HOMELAND, LIBERATE IT, RETURN TO IT AND EXERCISE THE RIGHT OF SELF-DETERMINATION IN IT. THIS RESPONSIBILITY EXTENDS TO ALL MILITARY, POLITICAL AND FINANCIAL MATTERS, AND ALL ELSE THAT THE PALESTINE ISSUE REQUIRES IN THE ARAB AND INTERNATIONAL SPHERES.

The addition here, as compared with the previous version, is that the organization assumes also the role of bringing into effect the regime it prefers after the victory.

ARTICLE 27) THE PALESTINE LIBERATION ORGANIZATION WILL COOPERATE WITH ALL ARAB STATES, EACH ACCORDING TO ITS CAPACITIES, AND WILL MAINTAIN NEUTRALITY IN THEIR MUTUAL RELATIONS IN THE LIGHT OF, AND ON THE BASIS OF, THE REQUIREMENTS OF THE BATTLE OF LIBERATION, AND WILL NOT INTERFERE IN THE INTERNAL AFFAIRS OF ANY ARAB STATE.

The obligation of neutrality, therefore, is not absolute but is qualified by the requirements of the battle of liberation.

ARTICLE 28) THE PALESTINIAN ARAB PEOPLE INSISTS UPON THE ORIGINALITY AND INDEPENDENCE OF ITS NATIONAL (*WATANIYYA*) REVOLUTION AND REJECTS EVERY MANNER OF INTERFERENCE, GUARDIANSHIP AND SUBORDINATION.

The Palestinian movement is not the tool for any Arab state and does not accept orders from any outside authority.

ARTICLE 29) THE PALESTINIAN ARAB PEOPLE POSSESSES THE PRIOR AND ORIGINAL RIGHT IN LIBERATING AND RESTORING ITS HOMELAND AND WILL DEFINE ITS POSITION WTH REFERENCE TO ALL STATES AND POWERS ON THE BASIS OF THEIR POSITIONS WITH REFERENCE TO THE ISSUE [OF PALESTINE] AND THE EXTENT OF THEIR SUPPORT FOR [THE PALESTINIAN ARAB PEOPLE] IN ITS REVOLUTION TO REALIZE ITS AIMS.

This is a new article, which includes a threat that the friendship of any state toward Israel will entail the enmity of the organization. A similar principle was established in the First Arab Summit Conference.

ARTICLE 30) THE FIGHTERS AND BEARERS OF ARMS IN THE BATTLE OF LIBERATION ARE THE NUCLEUS OF THE POPULAR ARMY, WHICH WILL BE THE PROTECTING ARM OF THE GAINS OF THE PALESTINIAN ARAB PEOPLE.

In other words, there is a future in the fedayeen or military career.

ARTICLE 31) THIS ORGANIZATION SHALL HAVE A FLAG, OATH AND ANTHEM, ALL OF WHICH WILL BE DETERMINED IN ACCORDANCE WITH A SPECIAL SYSTEM.

ARTICLE 32) TO THIS COVENANT IS ATTACHED A LAW KNOWN AS THE FUNDAMENTAL LAW OF THE PALESTINE LIBERATION ORGANIZATION, IN WHICH IS DETERMINED THE MANNER OF THE ORGANIZATION'S FORMATION, ITS COMMITTEES, INSTITUTIONS, THE SPECIAL FUNCTIONS OF EVERY ONE OF THEM AND ALL THE REQUISITE DUTIES ASSOCIATED WITH THEM IN ACCORDANCE WITH THIS COVENANT.

ARTICLE 33) THIS COVENANT CANNOT BE AMENDED EXCEPT BY A TWO-THIRDS MAJORITY OF ALL THE MEMBERS OF THE NATIONAL COUNCIL OF THE PALESTINE LIBERATION ORGANIZATION IN A SPECIAL SESSION CALLED FOR THIS PURPOSE.